THE 12 POINTS OF POWER

A Step-by-Step Guide
to Overcoming Addictive Patterns
and Limiting Beliefs

THE 12 POINTS OF POWER

A Step-by-Step Guide
to Overcoming Addictive Patterns
and Limiting Beliefs

SHERMAN HARGRAVE

FOREWORD
BY BRIAN WALTON

Park Point
PRESS

Park Point Press | 573 Park Point Drive | Golden CO 80401

Copyright 2021, Sherman Hargrave

All rights reserved.
No part of this book may be reproduced in any form without permission in writing from the publisher, except for brief quotations embodied in critical articles or reviews.

Park Point Press
573 Park Point Drive
Golden, CO 80401-7402
720-496-1370

www.csl.org/en/publications/books
www.scienceofmind.com/publish-your-book

Printed in the United States of America
Published July 2021

Editor: Julie Mierau, JM Wordsmith
Design/Layout: Maria Robinson, Designs On You, LLC

ISBN ebook: 978-0-917849-95-4
ISBN paperback: 978-0-917849-94-7

We live in a Universe of

Ever-Expanding Good,

in which life is always on our side

to do wonderful and incredible things.

Our responsibility is

to stay in the flow of this

Ever-Expanding Good.

FOREWORD

I first saw Sherman Hargrave in 2004 at a service of the Agape International Spiritual Center, a trans-denominational community in Los Angeles based on "Ageless Wisdom-New Thought" principles. Sherman was one of the ushers helping people find places to sit in the 1,400-plus seat sanctuary. We didn't speak. I did, however, find myself drawn to watch him. There was something compelling about the way he went about his task. Unsurprisingly, he was being a kind, friendly, helpful, and effective usher, but I saw something more. He seemed to radiate a magnetic goodness and decency by which people were uplifted.

Over time, as we both continued attending Agape, we continued to learn about each other. Then, one Friday night, we were both surprised to find ourselves sitting across from the other in a meeting outside of Agape and to learn we were both in recovery. He had nearly twenty years and I but a few. Sherman grew up in Newark, New Jersey, and left its rough streets for years in the U.S. Navy, became established as a chef, and had his own restaurant and catering business. In the process he went through addiction to recovery and then to deeper spiritual understandings and experiences. I had been a lawyer for 30 years, a union executive and negotiator in the entertainment industry, and served on a number of boards of nonprofits.

As the years went by, we both took several classes and programs at Agape and elsewhere and grew our spiritual practices. Sherman mastered New Thought-Ageless Wisdom principles and studied at the University of Metaphysics. He continued to share and teach spiritual principles in several venues. I became an Agape Licensed Spiritual Practitioner and earned a master's degree in spiritual psychology at the University of Santa Monica. We kept in contact over the years and worked together in the Agape Prison Ministry, to which Sherman made milestone contributions.

Now Sherman has written this powerful book.

I invite you to look at spiritual transformation as a mountain that has no summit. If we work at it, we can just keep going higher and higher. Sherman has done that. His one-day-at-a-time spiritual practices led to his recovery. His story and spiritual inquiry, however, didn't end there.

He followed a call from within to a subsequent years-long deeper spiritual journey and a successful search for his life's purpose. The central one he found, as he writes here, is a spiritual imperative for him to "remind myself and others that life is expecting wonderful and marvelous things from each and every one of us." This book is about that. It is compelling evidence that

Sherman put that imperative into action. He continued to go higher—and here he shares that with us.

The 12 Points of Power is universal and personal. It is universal in that Sherman sets forth spiritual principles and laws that govern the universe, that are transformational, and that are available to all. It is personal in that he describes and invites each of us to a personal experience of transforming spiritual practices, which he illustrates by letting the reader in on his own experiences. Some of his experiences are remarkable, dramatic, and surprising. I found them moving to read. He has practiced what he preaches. Some might find one or more of these personal experiences shocking. Sherman's life was no walk in the park. Importantly, though, his very openness about his experiences demonstrates his freedom, strength, generosity, and quiet fearlessness.

Those qualities stem from Sherman knowing he is not just a collection of his experiences. He has replaced earlier limiting beliefs with the truth about who he is. And it is that truth about ourselves that will set us free.

The New Thought-Ageless Wisdom principles upon which this book is based are found in various forms in many religious and spiritual traditions going back to some Greek philosophers and including Judaism, Islam, the Sufi mystics, Christianity and Buddhism, among others. They are also consistent with aspects of some psychological schools of thought.

Seeing oneself within the context of these principles is

powerful and liberating. Although intellectual understanding is a good beginning, it is not enough. Spiritual practices (meditation, affirmative prayer, affirmations, service) are required to build our awareness and create the powerful experiences available to us. Ultimately, our oneness with the Spirit is experiential. Sherman assists us in that endeavor throughout the book and gives us affirmations for each day of the week at the end of each chapter.

A spiritual counselor once asked me what floated my boat in life, what turned me on, what excited me. After some thought, I told him that what turns me on is seeing people come to realize that they are fundamentally OK and that they can let all of their limiting beliefs about themselves melt away in the warmth of the truth of who and whose they are. That experience, that epiphany, is spiritually tectonic and gives an unparalleled birth of freedom and joy. I have had some of those experiences myself and wish them for all. I am honored to have written the foreword for this book because reading it could well lead to such a new birth for those who absorb it.

Sherman Hargrave has written a powerful book. He is well and uniquely qualified to have done so. He well knows that about which he writes.

The 12 Points of Power is for anyone struggling with any form of addiction, whether to substances of any kind or to any recurring behaviors that disturb their peace and keep them restricted in any way. Furthermore, I recommend this book

FORWARD

to any gratefully recovering addicts with recovery time who are open to a journey to a deeper understanding of themselves and spiritual matters that can lead to more vibrant and liberated living. Finally, even if you have never personally experienced addiction, this book will illuminate spiritual truths and deepen empowering spiritual awareness for you, too.

Peace and blessings to all.

Brian Walton
Agape Licensed Spiritual Practitioner
Los Angeles

DEDICATION

This book is dedicated to all those who decided to never ever give up on life—for life will never ever give up on you.

In working every day with others who have given up on their dreams and aspirations, I've come into the awareness that there is a mandate on my life. As one who has overcome twenty years of the horrors of alcohol and drug addiction, it is imperative to remind myself and others that life is expecting wonderful and marvelous things from each and every one of us.

No matter how many times we have fallen down in this process of life, the ground is no place for an expression of the Most High.

We are living in a truly wonderful time to be alive. Modern technology continues to evolve as it enhances our lives, and people are more spiritually evolved than ever before, as a result of discovering a Deeper Love Within ourselves.

Thy will is being done, and Thy kingdom has come right here on Earth, through the expression of those who have found this new way of life.

PREFACE

This book of my life experiences—and the experiences of others who have learned to practice these spiritual principles in all of their affairs—is set up to assist readers in using this scientific and spiritual method of renewing our minds and dealing with our emotions.

In the following pages, you will find twelve chapters, each focusing on a specific Point of Power. At the end of each chapter, you will find seven Affirmations of Truth, one for each day of the week. They are designed to remind us of the mighty "I Am" Presence within, waiting to express Itself as us. If possible, you will want to stand up while speaking these affirmations aloud, for maximum effect. I also recommend that you put these affirmations on your cell phone, laptop, desktop, a good old three-by-five card, or anyplace you will see them throughout the course of your day.

Seeing and speaking these affirmations aloud—at least three times a day—will consciously connect you to the Deeper Love that lies within you. The practice of this method introduces us to a fantastically new and exciting way of seeing ourselves and the world we live in.

Throughout the book, I use a variety of names for God. You'll see me refer to the Deeper Love Within, Overflow of Life and other terms by which I mean God. You'll recognize them by their capital letters.

My prayer is for you to begin using and expressing these new ways of overcoming addictive patterns that have been holding you hostage, and in doing so, begin living from a fearless Overflow of Life.

ACKNOWLEDGEMENTS

I gratefully acknowledge the people in my recovery process who steadfastly stood by me in my most difficult time—as well as in my good times—in this process of life. Thank you to those loving souls who believed in me when I couldn't believe in myself.

Thank you to the U.S. Navy for sending me through alcohol and drug rehabilitation two times, when most people would have only been given one chance.

Thank you to my mother, Elaine Hargrave, who always held me up through her loving prayers, especially when I needed those prayers the most and didn't even know it.

Thank you to my son, Ahmad, for the joy he has given me by showing up on this planet.

I also have a deep sense of gratitude for Narcotics Anonymous for introducing me to the "real me" beyond the outside substances that stood in the way of knowing myself and others at a deeper level for so long.

I would also like to thank Michael Bernard Beckwith and the Agape International Spiritual Center for all of its many classes in spiritual growth and development.

Thank you to those who encouraged me to write a book when I thought I didn't have a book to write—to Kimberly McGinnis for keeping me on point, Idris Hester for the fine tuning, and William Roper for his support.

AUTHOR'S NOTE

While sitting in the office of Sherman's Cajun and Creole Buffet restaurant counting the receipts from our profits for that day, I heard that still small voice within asking, "Is this all there is to life?"

I was running a successful restaurant and, out of nowhere, this question came to me. It would lead me on a search for the deeper meaning of life. A divine discontent for the way things were going had set in, and like so many others before me who have come from a sense of lack and limitation, I had been looking for things outside of me to fill that void—only to find out that life is an inside job.

My hope is to share my journey with others through this book, and in doing so, inspire my readers to tap into this Deeper Love Within. This ever-emerging good lies at the core and essence of who we are, as I and so many before me have gratefully discovered.

TABLE OF CONTENTS

FOREWORD vii
DEDICATION xiii
PREFACE xv
ACKNOWLEDGEMENTS xvii
AUTHOR'S NOTE xix
CHAPTER **1** — **POWER** **3**
    Infinite Intelligence 5
    The Miracle Happens 6
    The "I Am" 8
    Daily Affirmations of Truth: POWER 11
CHAPTER **2** — **BELIEFS** **13**
    Universal Conspiracy for Good 15
    The Overcoming 16
    Subconscious Mind 19
    Daily Affirmations of Truth: BELIEFS 21
CHAPTER **3** — **LETTING GO** **23**
    Change 25
    A New View of Life 27

Self-Acceptance 30
Daily Affirmations of Truth: LETTING GO 32

CHAPTER 4 — **FAITH** **35**
Overcoming Fear 37
Getting Out of Our Comfort Zones 39
Use Faith as a Starting Point 41
Welcome to the Next Stage 44
Daily Affirmations of Truth: FAITH 46

CHAPTER 5 — **PRAYER** **49**
In the Beginning Was the Word 51
Lifting the Consciousness 52
The Breakthrough 53
The Next Stage of Evolution 55
Daily Affirmations of Truth: PRAYER 58

CHAPTER 6 — **DECISIONS** **61**
Starting Point 63
The Inner Opening 64
The Conscious Decision 65
Daily Affirmations of Truth: DECISIONS 68

CHAPTER 7 — **FORGIVENESS** **71**
Responsibility 73
Freedom to Change 75

    Blame Throwers 76

    Self-Forgiveness 78

    Love Thyself 79

    Daily Affirmations of Truth: FORGIVENESS 82

CHAPTER **8** — **UNCONDITIONAL LOVE** **85**

    Love Loves to Love 87

    The Intention to Love 88

    Daily Affirmations of Truth: UNCONDITIONAL LOVE . . . 93

CHAPTER **9** — **GRATEFULNESS** **95**

    Lessons and Blessings 97

    An Opening for the Gifts 99

    The Practice 100

    Daily Affirmations of Truth: GRATEFULNESS 102

CHAPTER **10** — **MINDFUL MEDITATION** **105**

    Be Still and Know that I Am 107

    An Inside Job 107

    Know Thyself 109

    Daily Affirmations of Truth: MINDFUL MEDITATION . . . 113

CHAPTER **11** — **CREATIVE VISUALIZATION** **115**

    Believing Is Seeing 117

    The Revelation 118

    The Inner Vision 119

Daily Affirmations of Truth:
CREATIVE VISUALIZATION 122

CHAPTER **12 — GIVING BACK** **125**

Courage to Change 127

In Service to Others 129

Daily Affirmations of Truth: GIVING BACK 132

AFTERWORD 135

ABOUT THE AUTHOR 136

THE 12 POINTS OF POWER

A Step-by-Step Guide
to Overcoming Addictive Patterns
and Limiting Beliefs

CHAPTER 1

POWER

"We acknowledge to our innermost selves that we are powerful beyond our wildest imagination and that we control our own destiny based on our new states of consciousness."

~ POINT OF POWER 1

"It takes courage to endure the sharp pains of self-discovery, rather than choose to take the dull pain of unconsciousness that would last the rest of our lives."

~ MARIANNE WILLIAMSON

Infinite Intelligence

Mental institutions, prisons, treatment centers, and hospitals are full to capacity with people who have given up on themselves and the power they have to control their lives. Millions of dollars find their way into the hands of pharmaceutical companies and illegal drug dealers every day because many have given up on their ability to master their emotions, over which we should have full control and power.

Your Point of Power is your awareness of a Deeper Love and Power within you. There is an infinite field of Universal Intelligence and Love that freely guides us, that is centered at the core and essence of everything ever created.

As spiritual beings having a human experience, we have complete access to this Universal Love and Intelligence to use as we see fit. Our minds are extensions of this Infinite Mind or Infinite Intelligence, and our hearts are extensions of this Universal Love. We are limited only by our human belief systems, which we have set up for ourselves based on fear and unconsciousness.

Can we truly say we are using this Universal Love and Intelligence when we are constantly caught up in fear, worry, and doubt? Or ingesting toxic waste (drugs, unhealthy foods, and alcohol) into our bodies? Or when we constantly shop to fill a void that only the awareness of our Deeper Love Within can permanently fill? Or having sex with someone for whom you have no loving feelings just to mask the loneliness of the moment?

We have always used Creative Intelligence to create our experiences. There are no coincidences. We are where we are today in life based on where we are in consciousness or unconsciousness. This Infinite Power constantly pushes forward for the universal expression of a Deeper Love to show up in our lives through all humankind.

The Deeper Love Within you is the same power that holds the planets in orbit and directs the seasons to change exactly when they're supposed to. This eternal Power and Love is the same Power and Love that flows through you and me, cut off only by our fear, worry, and doubt.

Any manifestation of Universal Intelligence or Infinite Love would have to be, by law, infinitely intelligent and infinitely loving. Therefore, since you were created in the image and likeness of this Love and Intelligence, you also contain these very qualities within you.

The Miracle Happens

How many times have we heard it said about someone who has managed to get clean or who has overcome any addictive behaviors after a few years, "What a miracle that person is!" In reality, the miracle is that anyone would make an unintelligent decision coming from a Source of Universal Intelligence.

Within us lies the starting point for love, peace, beauty, power, and intelligent decisions. We activate these spiritual qualities by becoming mindful and aware of the words we speak, the thoughts we entertain, and the actions we take throughout the course of our day.

This Deeper Love Within has been given many names: God, Spirit, Allah, Christ, Buddha, Atman, Higher Power, and many more. Jesus called it the Kingdom of God within you. We are not so much concerned with Its names as we are with Its nature. Unfortunately, humans have unconsciously created a God in their own image and likeness—one who needed anger management from time to time or a God who gives and takes away life. We are told, "It is not the Father's will that any of His children should perish, but that they should have life and have it abundantly." This is the unconditional universal Deeper Love Within I am referring to.

Some people want to see God as something outside of themselves—a power that is cut from a different cloth—failing to realize that we are all One with this Father/Mother Love Presence. We are here to acknowledge this omnipotent, omniscient, and omnipresent Deeper Love in all things, as all things, in its entirety.

Ralph Waldo Emerson reminds us, "We are inlets and can become outlets to all there is in God." As the very individualization of God, we are students on a quest to become consciously connected to our Deeper Love Within. We are here to push ourselves to release this indwelling love, peace, and beauty that lies as the foundation of who and what we are in essence and substance.

By incorporating into our lives the spiritual principles laid out in this book, we begin to see ourselves as the Universe sees us, knowing that the Universe sees us as perfect, whole, and complete.

Our Point of Power is our awareness of a Higher Power within us, showing up as spiritually inspired and driven human beings who have come to see ourselves as more than alcoholics and addicts, more than disabled veterans, more than consumers, more than any other self-defeating titles we have chosen to live down to.

To those of you who have been looking for a way to comfortably contemplate and converse on the truth about life from a higher state of consciousness—rather than identifying with character flaws from your past—I welcome you.

The "I Am"

We are always consciously or unconsciously setting the standards for our lives based on our self-identification. Every "I am" that comes out of our mouth must manifest itself ultimately into feelings or form—sometimes both.

Every "I am sick," "I am always broke," "I am always lonely," or "I am an addict," sets the stage for more to follow. When you say and feel "I am," you are releasing the eternal Flow of Life to express Itself as that which follows your "I am." In other words, "I am" is the activity of God expressing Itself in all of our affairs.

"As a man thinketh in his heart, so is he." This is the law of cause and effect. Every man and every woman is a law unto themselves, and we activate this law by the words we speak and the thoughts we entertain.

As powerful servants of the Love of Life, we can give our lives over to the care of love, peace, and beauty—instead of hosting self-defeating concepts of ourselves passed down by others, coming from a place of fear and unconsciousness.

Many of us on this path to having life and having it more abundantly have had inner visions of walking into fellowship rooms and meeting halls of spiritual growth and development. The flow of our identification of "I am peace," "I am radiant life," "I am truth," "I am prosperity" echoed throughout the walls, and our daily conversations forever set the wheels in motion to enjoy life beyond our wildest imagination. The time is *now* to act from these inner promptings.

On this journey you will come to know yourself at a deeper level, being challenged to see yourself and others as the Universe sees you—the offspring of its very whole and loving nature. There is a calling to see and express ourselves through this higher vision of Love, from the same light of the enlightened ones who have come before us and are with us now. Your life is to also become a declaration of bliss, joy, and ecstasy.

Life is a conditioning process and we are always being conditioned by outside forces unless we have found a way of listening to the Deeper Love Within us. As the saying goes, "If you don't have a plan for yourself, someone else has got one for you."

This is why the Apostle Paul warned us, "Be ye not transformed by the world but by the renewing of your mind." By systematically using affirmative prayers and resting in the inner silence (meditation), you will begin to take control of your own way of thinking and life, thus setting the tone for Ever-Expanding Good to show up as you.

Every architect or clothes designer must resort back to the original blueprint or pattern when their building or production does not go according to plan. As spiritual beings here to be the activity of love, peace, and intelligence, it only makes sense that we take the time and effortless effort to fall back into the spiritual blueprint of love, peace, and intelligence. Your affirmative prayers and statements of truth are to remind you of how divine and magnificent you truly are.

As someone who has overcome twenty years of the horrors of alcohol and drug addiction, cancer, massive asthma attacks, bankruptcy—and who has been free from addiction for the last thirty-four years—I want to believe I truly have earned the right to write about this wonderfully new and exciting way to see life.

DAILY · AFFIRMATIONS · OF · TRUTH

POINT OF **1** *POWER*

POWER

DAY 1

I acknowledge to my innermost self that there is a Power and Presence within me that is powerful beyond my greatest expectations. *And so it is!*

DAY 2

I am an expression of Universal Power flowing through me, making all things possible in my life. *And so it is!*

DAY 3

I am created in the image and likeness of the Power of Love, allowing me to love like I've never loved before. *And so it is!*

DAY 4

There is an Infinite Power that stands knocking at the door of my soul, waiting to guide me with Its powerful presence. *And so it is!*

POINT OF 1 POWER

DAY 5

The Power of God surrounds me, upholds me, guides me, and protects me. For this I am eternally grateful. *And so it is!*

DAY 6

I am pure Spirit and Power, and there is a spiritual and powerful aspect of me that has never been hurt, harmed, or endangered. *And so it is!*

DAY 7

In my powerful new state of Higher Consciousness, I live, move, and have my peaceful and eternal being. *And so it is!*

BELIEFS

"We stand firm in the belief that there is a perfect and Deeper Love Within us that is constantly conspiring for our good."

~ POINT OF POWER 2

"All I have seen teaches me to trust the Creator for all I have not seen."

~ RALPH WALDO EMERSON

Universal Conspiracy for Good

We live in a universe governed by laws: spiritual laws, mental laws, mathematical laws, laws of gravity, and so on. In this process, our greatest attention is to be placed on the spiritual and mental laws of life—it is the way in which we use these laws that determines the quality of our lives.

The first law of life is the law of harmony, which simply proves that everything is in divine and perfect order. As evidence of this Universal Support System, which is constantly waiting to express Itself for the good of all, Dr. Cressy Morrison shares an amazing study of eels and their spawning process in his book, *Man Does Not Stand Alone*.

Every year, eels from all over the world set out on a journey to a particular part of the Atlantic Ocean to spawn. Nature slows down the birthing process so every one of the eels arrives at its destination at the same time—no matter how far it may have come from—before they all give birth to their little ones.

After spawning and returning to their original locations, these particular eels will not be seen anywhere other than their places of origin. This is amazing evidence of a Universal Conspiracy for Good, working as the law of harmony.

We are told, "My God shall supply your every need according to His riches in glory," which is God's nature. This nature of a Deeper Love Within gives us the gift of peace, power, spirit, life, and abundance, even in our most trying times.

The Universe (God) has supplied us with the seed substance of love so we may become the greatest lovers the world has ever known. We each have the potential to express the same great Unconditional Love Mother Teresa exemplified through our acts and deeds of Unconditional Love flowing from a higher state of consciousness. There is a Christ potential at the core and essence of each one of us, awaiting our recognition. "Before they call, I will answer" (Isaiah 65:24).

We open the door to these infinite possibilities of life by the things we focus on, followed by the belief that all things are possible in our lives. This is the basis for the understanding of the law of attraction.

Don't get me wrong when I say all things are possible, but I should add that they are possible only if you truly believe they are possible.

The Overcoming

On Christmas Day 1984, I had my right kidney removed due to a cancerous tumor my doctors discovered while I was on active duty in the U.S. Navy. Then only two days after the surgery, I had illegal heroin delivered to my hospital room at Balboa Naval Hospital in San Diego, California. I began wheeling my IV set-up around, with my ass hanging out of the back of one of those designer gowns they give you, looking for some privacy to inject the heroin through my IV cord and into my body.

I was so down on myself for getting this far into drug addiction that I began to give up on life and I continued to intravenously use drugs for the next eight months after the surgery. I was committing suicide on the installment plan, culminating in a twenty-year bout with drug addiction.

On August 3, 1985, I stood looking at myself in a full-length mirror with tears running down my face. They were tears of disappointment and disparity as to the direction my life had taken. I thought about the people I had let down time after time, the people I had stolen from and manipulated, not to mention how I had let myself down.

That Still Small Voice Within began to remind me that I am more than that which I was expressing at the time. This face-to-face encounter with the man in the mirror allowed me to move beyond my fears and disappointments and self-putdowns to check myself into the U.S. Navy Rehabilitation program for the second time in a four-year period.

While detoxing my body and mind in an alcohol and drug treatment center—and going through a rough time of being with myself both physically and mentally—I was given a Bible passage at a twelve-step meeting by a complete stranger who saw the fear and desperation I was going through.

This passage, Mark 11:23, reads, "Whosoever... shall not doubt in his heart, but shall believe that those things which he saith shall come to pass, he shall have whatsoever he saith."

Not being a biblically based or religious person at the time, and being opposed to any organized religion, I just threw this Bible passage to the side on my dresser and paid no attention to it.

Mystically, I began to remember these powerful words while going through a vigorous mini-boot camp during the drug treatment process. I began to embrace other people's faith and belief in me until I could believe in myself. I was eventually aided by these magical and mystical words, and I began to believe that I, too, could start to recover, one day at a time.

While going through a difficult time in treatment and wanting to leave from time to time, I was reminded, "Why destroy your life today by leaving this treatment center?" I was being prompted by destructive fear-based thought patterns, failing to realize at the time that everything is subject to change.

Life has taught me over the years that it's just as easy to go online and study the great experiences of those who have overcome sickness, poverty, prejudice, and addictions as it is to start studying the different cancers that exist when your doctor tells you that you have a cancerous tumor—but the former approach is much more exciting and empowering.

We put the great laws of healing and love into action through our higher states of consciousness, our thoughts, and our words. Our words govern our demonstration, and once we accept that healing is possible, all spiritual and personal breakthroughs begin with this change in our beliefs.

The great life coach Anthony Robbins says, "We are driven

by two emotions in our life: the need to avoid pain or to gain pleasure." Robbins goes on to say, "The most effective way to change is to get your brain to associate massive pain to your old disempowering beliefs and actions, and tremendous pleasure to your new and empowering beliefs and actions."

Many have been conditioned by societal norms to believe that if we make massive amounts of money and have the right partners and houses, our lives will be complete—only to read about some mega stars who also believed this, acquired great financial wealth, and still took their own lives.

The problem is when these partners leave you or the money runs out, some sort of depression sets in. This happens because we have built our foundations and beliefs on shifting sands, instead of on solid spiritual principles. Our attachment to these beliefs caused us to suffer more than anything else, for life truly is an inside job.

When we come to seek first the kingdom of God, all else shall be added. This kingdom is your conscious connection to the Deeper Love Within you, and you will come to know that all your spiritual needs have always been met. Freedom from addictions of any kind is your loving divine birthright.

Subconscious Mind

The subconscious mind is a collection of everything we have come to believe in our lives, whether fact or fiction, truth or lies.

It's been my personal experience—and the experience of many others—that people with addictive personalities will come to rationalize the most insane nonsense until nonsense begins to make good sense as to why we continue to practice our addictive behaviors.

As we begin to see living examples of people who have overcome the horrors of addiction, followed by a powerful will to change more than we want to stay the same, we can begin to recondition the subconscious mind.

It was only through an honest inventory of this insane nonsense in my life, preceded by the willingness to change, that I began to renew my mind. The happiness and despair in my life has depended on one thing and one thing only: what I have conditioned myself to believe about the meaning of life.

The ultimate quest in this creative process of life is to become consciously aware that we are co-creating our own lives, that we are the masters of our own fates and the captains of our own souls, limited only by the limitations we have placed on ourselves.

It's been said that, as human beings, we have more than 30,000 thoughts a day, most of them being negative and repetitive. In this conditioning process, we are either conditioning ourselves to believe that life is for us and never against us, or we are conditioning ourselves to believe that we have nothing coming our way. The Affirmations of Truth established in this book have a scientific way of reconditioning your subconscious mind so that you may have life and have it abundantly.

DAILY · AFFIRMATIONS · OF · TRUTH

POINT OF 2 POWER

BELIEFS

DAY ❶

Knowing that it is done unto me as I believe, I express feelings of love, beauty, and intelligence, moment by moment, and watch them show up everywhere I go. *And so it is!*

DAY ❷

I believe with all of my heart and soul there is a Universal Conspiracy that is constantly conspiring for the good of all. *And so it is!*

DAY ❸

The belief that my body is the activity of perfect health and wholeness allows me to live my life with zest, zeal, vigor, and vitality. *And so it is!*

DAY ❹

In viewing life from the eyes of Unconditional Love, I see

POINT OF 2 POWER

and believe the very best in every situation I encounter, and in every person I meet throughout the course of my day. *And so it is!*

DAY 5

My belief from a consciousness of Infinite Intelligence, Vibrant Health, and Unconditional Love allows me to open the door to these spiritual gifts of Life. *And so it is!*

DAY 6

Hidden away within me is a vast treasure of Infinite Power, Infinite Peace, and so much more. I open my heart and soul to this new belief system, thus releasing my gifts to the world. *And so it is!*

DAY 7

My life is a belief and out-picturing of abundance and prosperity, knowing and believing that even before I ask, it has already been given to me. *And so it is!*

CHAPTER 3

LETTING GO

"From this new Deeper Love Within, we are constantly involved in the practice of letting go of any and all thoughts of separation, cleverly disguised as fear."

~ POINT OF POWER 3

"In the end, only three things matter: how much you love, how gently you live, and how gracefully you let go of things not meant for you."

~ BUDDHA

Change

The greatest part of what I have learned in my life has been the unlearning of the fear-based lies I have told myself. They were passed down by others over the years, and believe me, there were many lies I had to unlearn.

As a kid growing up in Newark, New Jersey—at the age of about six years old—I experienced a hurricane that forced the schools to close early for the day to get everyone home safely.

As the thunder and lightning began to intensify, I was so frightened that I remember hiding under the bed in fear. My sister, who was a few years older than me was, in the room at the time, and I asked her to explain the thunder and lightning. She told me that they were a sign from God that He was pissed off, and it was His way of talking.

This, coupled with the sound of trees falling on cars and all sorts of other destruction the hurricane left behind, in my mind seemed to be irrefutable evidence that God was, in fact, pissed off.

In addition, when my sister would leave the house from time to time while we were growing up, I would ask her where she was going. She would respond by telling me that she was "going to hell" if she didn't start praying soon.

Now, I understand today that she was probably just passing down some witty clichés to keep me out of her business—but at the time I didn't realize that these clichés were beginning to mold my belief system as to how I viewed God and life.

The problem with a life based in fear is that once we begin to accept these erroneous clichés or the limiting beliefs of others as truth, they become ingrained into our subconscious mind as truth. The subconscious mind, being the memory bank of anything and everything we have accepted as truth, can't take a joke—even if it may have been intended as a joke.

As a result of my distorted teachings, I never felt much like going to church, although I was dragged there (figuratively speaking) every Sunday morning. My role models in life growing up in the streets of Newark and East Orange, New Jersey, were con artists and drug dealers. I just happened to fall under the tutoring of some people who had a limited perception of life, a life based in fear rather than in love.

These con artists, hustlers, and drug dealers were personally instructed by my brother—while he himself was locked away in jail—to take care of me. These people took a liking to me and showed me more love than I was receiving at home, and thus I began the journey of going in and out of juvenile detention centers at the age of eleven. This was my introduction to drugs, alcohol, and crime.

Children of this age carefully watch what's going on in their surroundings and begin to take on the wisdom—and the ignorance—of others who influence them most. This careful observation sends messages to the subconscious mind, resulting in our teachers' behaviors becoming our own. In my case, I concluded that this is how the game of life is played.

In this street life, I was taught early on not to show any outward feeling of love toward anyone, for it would be a sign of weakness and used against me later. What I didn't understand at the age of eleven (and a few years later) is that most of these role models in my life came from extremely abusive and uninformed families. They set the tone for the distorted belief systems based in fear that would become my way of life.

I was one of the fortunate ones who made it out of this limited and limiting environment, set up by faulty belief systems. I escaped to the U.S. Navy some years later to avoid going to jail and prison as an adult. Fortunately, I have spent the last thirty-four years of my life taking inventory and reexamining those erroneous beliefs and helping others to do the same.

A New View of Life

Those of you who have broken away from the limited views of the past by now know that we are connected to a Power and Love far greater than our past beliefs and experiences. I want to welcome you to a new and exciting way of seeing ourselves and the world we live in.

Perhaps you've seen others who have overcome past limitations based on their own life stories. Know that we are all capable of doing the same and so much more. This is because we are all created in the image and likeness of a Deeper Love Within.

In this metaphysical approach to a tremendously new and exciting way of seeing ourselves and the world we live in, we must accept and take 100 percent responsibility for our lives. We must get out of the blame game. Whether it is getting out of that prehistoric crutch of blaming the devil or the New Age crutch of blaming our parents and our past, blaming is blaming.

In cleansing the subconscious mind of those old worn-out stories of what happened to us in the past, we will find it invigorating and exciting to talk and think about where we are going—but more importantly, where we are in the moment—instead of where we came from.

There really is no end to the limitless possibilities of life when we learn to let go of those sick ideas that no longer serve us, no matter how rational these ideas may seem to ourselves or to others. Some people will suggest it's OK to drink if most of our problems have been centered on using drugs, or that we can still hang out in those same places with those same people who are doing the things we are trying to get away from.

Believe me, I have first-hand and immediate experience with this insanity. If you hang out with nine people who are operating from this fear-based way of thinking, you will be number ten.

In November 1984, two months before having my right kidney removed, I began experiencing excruciating pains in my side, followed by massive amounts of blood coming from my penis as I urinated. After checking into Balboa Naval Hospital, I began to convince myself that if I were to stop shooting crystal meth and go back to shooting heroin, these problems would go away. This is the kind of insane nonsense that begins to make good sense when we are caught up in addiction and are feeling a sense of separation from the Deeper Love Within ourselves.

So many are caught up in these limited perceptions based on where we came from in life, thus bringing these views into manifestation. And I was personally held captive by the limited beliefs of certain support groups early in my recovery, through my own ignorance of how the laws of perception work.

The belief that we cannot change our past, biology, or DNA is beginning to be challenged by scientific scholars engaged in cell-biology. According to world-renowned cell biologist Bruce Lipton, "Our perceptions have the power to change our genetic makeup. Your beliefs can and do control your biology."

Every man and woman is a law unto themselves. As long as we tell ourselves and others that we suffer from a disease for which there is no known cure, we are setting a law into motion to experience more sickness. "It is done unto you as you believe" (Matthew 8:13).

Every day that I verbally rehearsed the preambles of a limited view of life, I set the stage for those views to come into manifestation. Conversely, every major breakthrough I have experienced in my spiritual evolution has come as a result of getting out of my comfort zones and challenging myself to do something different, often going against my nervous system and the beliefs of others.

I have found that the things I benefited from most in my thirty-four years of recovery have usually been the things I didn't want to do. This leads me to believe in the old saying, "The winners do what they have to do, and the losers do what they want to do."

Early in my recovery someone brought it to my attention that every day of our lives, our experiences are based on the sum total of our beliefs about ourselves and the world we live in. I knew I had to let go of my old beliefs.

In learning to use our stories as stepping-stones to our next stage of evolution, rather than as setbacks, our stories can become our greatest transformational tools in freeing ourselves and others from our past beliefs and behaviors.

Self-Acceptance

I learned to accept all of my experiences from the past in order to appreciate them, acknowledge them as lessons and blessings, and move on. There is nothing that has happened to us, or that we have done to others in the past, that can prevent us from experiencing the beauty and love of today.

Our attitudes surrounding what life means to us—yesterday and today—will determine our experience in the future. If we perceive the very best, we shall receive even more of the very best.

Self-acceptance means coming into the realization that who we are in essence and substance shines so brightly that our past or our fears of the future have no more power over us. When we begin to adopt this new state of consciousness, we begin to live life with fresher and higher standards for ourselves and the world we live in.

No matter what seeming difficulties you face in your life, there is a Deeper Love Within you that is greater than anything you are experiencing. The awareness and acceptance of this Deeper Love can dissolve any fear-based thoughts you may have convinced yourself are real.

When we begin to shift our perceptions of who we are, the quality of our lives also begins to shift. When we see ourselves as expressions and the activity of a Deeper Love Within, we reap the benefits of what we have sown.

This new life that awaits us is heaven right here on Earth, based in a new state of consciousness. What we are inwardly spiritually rehearsing will become what we are humanly demonstrating, moment by moment.

Why not remind ourselves through affirmative prayers that "I Am the Deeper Love Within," "I Am the Light, I Am the Truth, I Am the Way," and "Beside this Deeper Love Within there is no other"?

DAILY · AFFIRMATIONS · OF · TRUTH

POINT OF ❸ POWER

LETTING GO

DAY ❶

I now let go of anything that could block my Deeper Love Within. I now express all of my God-given qualities, moment by moment. *And so it is!*

DAY ❷

Incredible spiritual growth and development continue to have their way with me as I let go of the past. *And so it is!*

DAY ❸

By letting go of all past thoughts, I experience the wonderful and amazing power of "now" flooding my body and soul. *And so it is!*

3—LETTING GO

DAY 4

My life is a constant process of letting go and letting the Presence of Love, Beauty, and Intelligence inform my experiences. *And so it is!*

DAY 5

As I continue to contemplate the facts of life from their highest points of view, I am now free from all fear, worry, and doubt. My life is good. *And so it is!*

DAY 6

As a child of God created in the image and likeness of Beauty, Bliss, and Love, I now release all thoughts contrary to this Universal Truth. *And so it is!*

DAY 7

In letting go of what happened to me, I am free to experience life from the Ever-Expanding Good of the Universe here and now. *And so it is!*

FAITH

*"We of ourselves can do nothing.
It is our faith in the Deeper Love Within that allows us
to do great things in the world."*

~ POINT OF POWER 4

*"Faith and fear both demand you believe
in something you cannot see.
You choose!"*

~ BOB PROCTOR

Overcoming Fear

While none of us can claim to express ourselves perfectly every day, there is a divine and perfect pattern of Love, Beauty, and Intelligence within each of us. We constantly use this pattern in co-creating everything that has ever been created in the world. It is the world according to you.

Jesus of Nazareth, in all of his spiritual awareness, confessed, "I of myself can do nothing. It is the Father within me that doeth the works" (John 5:30). As we come to the realization that we are here to amplify and glorify the Father/Mother God Presence within each of us—showing up as Love, Peace, Beauty, and Intelligence—our faith in a Higher Power within becomes the starting point for every world-changing endeavor we will ever accomplish.

Everyone who has overcome any addiction or limited way of viewing themselves and the world we live in adds to a higher collective state of consciousness of the world. This means that we truly are life's gifts to the world, for every time our consciousness is raised, we raise the consciousness of the world based on our demonstration.

My faith in others who have overcome addiction through this recovery process began with the clues left behind by the amazing warriors who came before me. We are in no way limited to this thing we call recovery. Be it drugs, alcohol, food, gambling, compulsive shopping, or sex, all addictions stem from a felt sense of separation from that Deeper Love Within. It is this separation that keeps us from living a fearless life, an affliction we all suffer with from time to time.

After getting a few years clean under my belt, I began to have a series of asthma attacks while I was still serving in the U.S. Navy. I noticed that each time I was admitted to the hospital—in which my stay usually lasted anywhere from six to eight days—spiritual revelations would begin to take place, revealing the next stage of consciousness in my life.

These revelations were always something greater for me than that which I could accept for myself, and they would occur right after the breakthrough of having my lungs open up. Before my lungs would open, I would feel like I was just about to die after hours and days of struggling to breathe. I would surrender, "Okay God, if this is how I'm supposed to die, I can accept this."

This may sound crazy to someone who hasn't had spiritual experiences like this. However, I began to go through isolated periods of pure bliss and ecstasy, as revelations and insights would come to me about how my life was to be lived. It was as if I had been strangulating the creative process within me by my worn-out beliefs that no longer served me. Now I was being called to let them go.

In retrospect, these asthma attacks became some of my biggest lessons and blessings in my journey of consciously connecting to the Deeper Love Within me. For example, there were times in my career and relationships when changes needed to be made, yet I didn't feel worthy because I was fearful as to how they would affect others. The Deeper Love Within allowed me to release my fears, step into my worthiness, and move forward with those changes.

While in the hospital—after letting go of the fears and going through these periods of bliss—I rarely wanted to see visitors because they would want to express their sympathy for me by asking things like, "What happened to you?", "Are you okay?", or "I was so worried about you." This would take me out of the rare moments of bliss and ecstasy I experienced during the breakthrough.

The nurses would often tell me that I was a breath of fresh air compared to the other patients they saw every day because of my overwhelming sense of gratitude for life, even while being hooked up to IVs, bottles, and my breathing apparatus.

The faith of coming out of two days of intensive care and surviving my last massive asthma attack allowed me to add to my spiritual resume, as proof of this Deeper Love Within that has never stopped working in my life.

Getting Out of Our Comfort Zones

After being in the U.S. Navy for ten years and clean for three years, I was released from the military on a medical discharge due to the continuation of my asthma attacks. During the next year I began to contemplate what I was going to do with my life.

Because I had been clean for three years, and my biggest role model was an alcohol and drug counselor, I discovered that the prerequisites for most counselors at the time were just to have a few years clean under their belt and the willingness to help others. This seemed like the safe and comfortable thing to do.

One year after being released from the U.S. Navy, I had another asthma attack, which resulted in my being hospitalized on the weekend I was scheduled to be one of the main speakers at a Narcotics Anonymous convention in San Diego. While in the hospital, I began to read a copy of *Ebony* magazine, and some would say that this was serendipity showing up in the TV lounge of the hospital—but I believe that it was a Deeper Love Within, showing itself anonymously once again in my life.

The magazine interviewed the top ten African American chefs in the United States, and six of these amazing chefs attended the prestigious Culinary Institute of America in Hyde Park, New York. I began to have faith that this same Universal Love acting on my behalf for my good—becoming clean and making it through those massive asthma attacks—would be the same power that would get me through the Culinary Institute of America and on to becoming a chef. And it did.

This same process of faith led me all the way to opening an award-winning Cajun and Creole Buffet in San Diego after graduating from the Culinary Institute.

These episodes of overcoming obstacle after obstacle, along with higher states of consciousness, would become the substance for my spiritual resume I was building for myself and others to fall back on when times seemed to be tough. As a result of this awareness, my inner muscle of faith began to grow.

Use Faith as a Starting Point

A man came to see Dr. Deepak Chopra some years ago complaining of a painful chest cough. X-rays revealed a large tumor between his lungs. They diagnosed the tumor as oat cell carcinoma, a deadly and fast-growing form of cancer. The man refused treatment, and Deepak lost track of him over the years.

Eight years later, a man came to see him with an enlarged lymph node in his neck, and it turned out to be oat cell carcinoma. Deepak realized it was the same man. They took chest x-rays and there was no trace of lung cancer. Normally, 99.99 percent of people with this condition would have died in six months, and 90 percent would not have lived that long, even with the maximum treatment. When asked what he did about his earlier bout of cancer, the man said he did nothing. He just decided that he was not going to let himself die of cancer and he refused treatment, thus going on to live much longer than anyone had thought was possible.

I have met people along the way in life who will tell you that faith and fear are the two starting points in consciousness—

and that there are some whose overwhelming faith seems to be centered in fear. This fear is so strong that they have fallen under the spell of a hypnotic state they call "Murphy's Law," which states that anything that can go wrong will go wrong. You don't want to be one in that number.

Faith is a principle that is always being used as the starting point for where we are in life. The question is what we have faith in or faith from. Faith in life and all of its infinite wonders and possibilities will always take us to places in a higher consciousness, demonstrating where the fear cannot go.

In other words, you can't serve two masters at the same time. We will never serve fear and a Deeper Love Within us simultaneously. Life's greatest gift to each of us is the freedom to choose, and as long as we are comfortable in our present state, we are not growing. We are here on this planet to expand and grow. Since change causes most people to become uncomfortable—and it is human nature to want to be comfortable—most of us will have to be brought to our knees, both figuratively and literally, to change our old self-defeating patterns.

While attending the Culinary Institute of America, I began to have trouble with culinary math, doubting myself and thinking I had a learning disorder (which seemed to be a popular term at the time). When I was in high school fifteen years earlier, I spent as little time as possible in classrooms. My priorities were selling drugs and chasing money and girls. So with this in mind, I made an appointment to see one of the guidance counselors at my chef school to discuss my self-diagnosed learning disorder.

After seeing the beautiful woman who was assigned to me two days before my appointment, my ego kicked in. I started to make excuses as to why I shouldn't go through with my appointment: "You are thirty-three years old, you should know this stuff by now." "Any chances of you ever dating this counselor will go out the window." "I don't even know this woman." I had to decide which was more important, saving my face or saving my ass. I chose the latter.

During the interview she asked me if I had a favorite sports team. I said yes, and she asked if I knew certain statistics of the team and its players. I began to rattle off certain statistics about the players and teams, which went onto dispel the notion of me having a learning disorder. Instead, my trouble was a lack of interest in math.

As I began to associate my success to learning and using culinary math as a path to creating amazing results in my future restaurant, those problematic math questions became easier to answer.

The point is that my comfort zone would have never let this woman empower me to move beyond my fears. After all, F.E.A.R. is an acronym for False Evidence Appearing Real.

When we allow ourselves to become vulnerable and to go where the fearful ones dare not go, we actually empower those who are asking to help us by giving them a sense of importance. One of the most challenging things in the process of recovery is having the courage to ask for help.

Welcome to the Next Stage

There is a Deeper Love and Power within each of us that is capable of doing for us that which our fears have stripped away. There is a built-in potential to think like Plato, Socrates, and Aristotle. It is our divine birthright to have a conscious connection with this Deeper Love, as Jesus, Buddha, Michael Bernard Beckwith, and countless others have had, based on their faith in the perfect love within.

Our responsibility is to have faith in Faith.

For those of you who find it uncomfortable to put yourself into the box of your old fear-based beliefs that no longer serve you, I welcome you to your next stage of spiritual growth and development. It is through our faith in this creative process of Life—and the willingness to release our concepts that have been overwhelmingly blocking our spiritual growth and development—that we will truly experience a freedom we never thought possible from those addictions. Our worn-out thoughts and beliefs will be sent back to the nothingness from which they came.

Reflect on a time when everything in your life seemed to be on point and you were at your happiest (substance free of course!). Your faith in those times will bring you into a greater happiness and will become the starting point for the joy you are entitled to experience in the here and now. This Deeper Love Within you is your innate ability and power to thrive and excel at anything you put your primary attention on—and your faith in—throughout the course of your day, each and every moment.

DAILY · AFFIRMATIONS · OF · TRUTH

POINT OF ❹ POWER

FAITH

DAY ❶

I'm so grateful and thankful for my faith in the spiritual awakening that I experience day by day as a result of my conscious connection to a Higher Power within. *And so it is!*

DAY ❷

I have tremendous faith in the Universal Conspiracy that conspires for my good and for the good of everyone. *And so it is!*

DAY ❸

There is a mighty flow of "I Am Joy," "I Am Bliss," and "I Am Ecstasy" flowing through every cell of my body, backed by my strong faith. *And so it is!*

DAY ❹

The mighty "I Am" Presence speaks into my heart daily, filling my heart and mind with faith in Its Divine Presence. *And so it is!*

DAY 5

I am so grateful to know that my faith continues to be the starting point for everything gloriously and abundantly showing up in my life. *And so it is!*

DAY 6

I am so thankful for the wonderful and powerful presence of this Deeper Love Within, expressing Itself as faith in everything I do. *And so it is!*

DAY 7

I am committed and dedicated to my faith in a Universe that is always on my side, expressing the ever-expanding Good of Life. *And so it is!*

CHAPTER 5

PRAYER

"We are to remind ourselves daily of our spiritual nature through the use of affirmative prayer and to make our Statements of Truth our foundation for living."

~ POINT OF POWER 5

"That which distinguishes the new thought from the old is not a denial of this Divine Reality, but an affirmation of its immediate availability."

~ ERNEST HOLMES

In the Beginning Was the Word

When we start with the premise that there is a Universal Support System conspiring for the good of all, we begin to live with the self-assurance that life is truly on our side, assisting us to express ourselves in dynamic ways. This Universal Support System reminds me of the biblical verses, "Before they call, I will answer," and "Behold, I stand at the door and knock."

Our responsibility is to learn how to activate this Infinite Power and Dynamic Force of Love through the powerful words we speak. We must also learn how to amplify the emotions behind those words, maintain a high state of consciousness, and surrender into the creative process of life.

When we consciously use our Affirmations of Truth, we deal with the essence and substance of things experienced in the here and now, based in principle and not in superstition. We are not dealing with a power that gives and takes away, but a Power that Is. Therefore, you are.

In this force field of Power and Love in which we live, move, and have our being, we are never more than a transcending breath and thought away from this powerful and all mighty "I Am" that we are.

In renewing our minds through our Affirmations of Truth —also known as affirmative prayers—we begin to think as the

Deeper Love Within would think, proclaiming, "I am the life and the way. I am the peace; I am the truth," thus activating these same God qualities within ourselves.

Every "I Am" coming out of your mouth is a statement of your truth, your affirmative prayer. It is this synchronization of the individual to the Universal Intelligence that makes each of us a vehicle for that which we are claiming. Every word spoken, if spoken with faith and conviction, must come back fulfilled and overflowing.

The problem is that most people are unconsciously speaking with faith and conviction about what they *don't* want to show up in their lives, instead of what they *do* want.

Lifting the Consciousness

We are told in Romans 12:2, "Be ye not transformed by the world, but by the renewing of your mind." It is in this awareness that we begin to set the tone for our lives and not let the outside world have it otherwise, for, we are in the world, but not of the world.

I use the terms affirmative prayer and Statements of Truth interchangeably, since every word we speak is a prayer, and all prayers are answered. As previously stated in Chapter 4, the questions become, "What are we praying for?" and "Where in our consciousness are we praying from?"

The most important purpose of our affirmative prayer is to

lift of our consciousness into a state where we remind ourselves that we are the activity of the Deeper Love Within, the extension of the Infinite Possibilities of Life magnifying and glorifying Itself in us, through us, and as us.

By cleansing our minds of the fear, worry, and doubts of the world, a whole new way of seeing ourselves and the world we live in—based on our conscious connection to the Deeper Love Within, which is our own love and power—becomes an opening for a more blissful and harmonious way of living.

The Breakthrough

One of the biggest breakthroughs in my spiritual growth came to me while doing the sixth step in a twelve-step program. With about fifteen years clean under my belt, I was asked to go back to my fourth step again and list all of my acquired defects of character such as shame, guilt, envy, jealousy, greed, lust, and so on.

These defects of character had set up a felt sense of separation from my Deeper Love Within. And I say a *felt* sense of separation for, in reality, we can never be separated from our Deeper Love Within. Just as the sun can never be separated from the light, we can never be separated from the omnipresence of our Deeper Love Within.

The sixth step of the twelve-step process asks that we "become entirely ready to have God remove all of our defects of character in our lives." Yet out of my higher state of consciousness, I had an "aha" moment. It became clear to me that if "the eyes of God are too pure to look upon evil" (Habakkuk 1:13)—meaning that the nature of love is such that there are no defects of character in the name and nature of love—God cannot remove that which goes against Its own nature. Just as the sun knows nothing of darkness, and the ocean knows nothing of dryness, love knows nothing of imperfection.

It becomes our responsibility to let go of those defects that no longer serve us in our spiritual growth and development. By letting go of shame, this defect is replaced by glory and honor, our God-given assets. Guilt is replaced by innocence, and we begin to see ourselves as the Universe sees us—perfect, whole and complete—as we activate this divine and perfect pattern of life.

Buddhist tradition talks about four "Divine Abodes," which are the qualities of an awakened mind. They are:

1. Loving Kindness   3. Appreciative Joy
2. Compassion   4. Equanimity

For example, in letting go of jealousy, we can begin to appreciate and participate in the joy and success of others. As I began to go down the list of all of my character defects that had become my way of operating in life, I was told to get a dictionary and find the opposite of these seventy-five defects of character, which were my God-given assets. I began to focus my attention on the assets as the very nature of who I am, more than I focused on the defects. In doing so, I began to realize the defects no longer had any legs to stand on. It then dawned on me that if I could discover a way to talk about and affirm the God-given qualities more than I talked about and affirmed the defects, there would no longer be any defects.

Science has proven that the things we put most of our attention on are what shows up in our lives. And while I was eternally grateful for all Narcotics Anonymous provided for me during my first twenty years of recovery, I had an indwelling urge that wouldn't allow me to continue to introduce myself as anything other than a child of God, created in Its own image and likeness. This was one of many major breakthroughs in my life.

I now believe I am more than an addict. I am here to be the very activity of Life—to express love, peace, spirit, truth, and every other God-given quality there is. The only limitations that exist in our lives are the ones we are claiming for ourselves.

The Next Stage of Evolution

The German poet-philosopher Johann Wolfgang Von Goethe reminds us in his teachings, "When we take a man as he is, we make him worse; but when we take a man as if he were already what he should be, we make him what he could be." Also, there is a principle of evolution that reminds us that those of us who are involved will continually evolve.

As the book *Basic Text of Narcotics Anonymous* states, "The time has come when the tired old lie 'Once an addict, always an addict' will no longer be tolerated by either society or the addict himself. We do recover." With my inner burning desire to express more than I had been expressing, I knew the days in my old paradigm paralysis—"Once an addict, always an addict"—were outnumbered.

There is an inner calling to know the truth that sets us free. This truth is activated by our affirmative prayers—those about ourselves and the world we live in. These Spiritual Affirmations become so forceful that the powerful words coming from our hearts with such high intensity are supported by the very laws of life. Our words become the fruits of the seed thoughts we plant, and by these fruits (the activity of our lives) people come to know us.

The fully awakened beings of the world will know the kind of thoughts you entertain by the peace and abundance you experience and express. Understanding and practicing this law of reaping and sowing become the cornerstone of our abundant living.

As students of truth on a spiritual path to freedom from the bondage of our past beliefs and lower states of consciousness, it become our personal declaration of independence to see prayer in the way in which Ralph Waldo Emerson saw prayer. He asked, "What is prayer but the contemplation of the facts of life from the highest points of view?"

Stop and contemplate these three affirmative prayers out loud for yourself right now:
1. God is Truth. There is a Truth within me that never wavers in spite of the conditions and circumstances of the world.
2. God is Life. My life is the Life of God. The Father/Mother Presence and I are One.
3. God is the Perfect Power within me.

We have the ability to start our lives all over again at any given moment. We activate a Deeper Love Within to express Itself in all our affairs by devoting ourselves to affirming the absolute Truth of who we are in substance and essence at least three times each day.

The most important times for planting new seed thoughts in the subconscious mind are when we get up in the morning and right before we go to bed at night. The subconscious mind, which is the receptor of everything we say and think, never sleeps. It does its best work in sending messages out to the Universal Mind (to be returned to us as we have sent them out) when we are in a relaxed state, spoken as One with a loving authority.

As a way of deeply empowering ourselves and activating our Deeper Love Within, we can write our own affirmative prayers, centered in the power of now. We are to pray as if our prayers are already done, not wishing or hoping but knowing they must return fulfilled.

DAILY · AFFIRMATIONS · OF · TRUTH

POINT OF 5 POWER

PRAYER

DAY 1

Every word I speak is a prayer representing the glory of God that I am grateful to give thanks for. *And so it is!*

DAY 2

My prayers are my deepest way of expressing my gratitude for the many blessings that continue to show up in my life. *And so it is!*

DAY 3

My prayer today is that I continue to be an opening for this mighty I Am Presence, which continues to knock at the door of my soul. *And so it is!*

DAY 4

My life is the out-picturing of my affirmative prayer of health and wholeness, which is radiating in every cell of my body. *And so it is!*

DAY 5

My prayers are a magnification of my gratitude for the comfort I experience in knowing that my life is the Life of God. *And so it is!*

DAY 6

I remain consciously inspired through affirmative prayer, and I welcome the Deeper Love Within me to shine and radiate. *And so it is!*

DAY 7

Just for today, I choose to pray and act as if it is already done from the will of the Divine and Perfect Pattern of Love within me. *And so it is!*

CHAPTER 6

DECISIONS

"We now make a decision to dedicate our consciousness to a Deeper Love Within, enabling us to think and live from a higher state of being."

~ POINT OF POWER 6

*"The universe has no fixed agenda.
Once you make any decision,
it works around that decision."*

~ ERNEST HOLMES

Starting Point

Where we are today in our relationships with others—our financial status, health and wholeness, and career aspirations—is a direct manifestation of where we are in consciousness. The decision to see the very best in everyone and every situation is the decision to be the Activity of Love expressing Itself as you.

After one year of being clean, I had one of many asthma attacks that opened me up to live my life with deeper meaning and purpose. Doctors spent two hours in the emergency room at Balboa Hospital in San Diego, trying to get my lungs opened up—then I was wheeled into a room with two older gentlemen who were patients along with me.

After struggling for nights to breathe—and praying one more time for God to get me out of this jam—something began to shift within me. Right praying would have been asking the Deeper Love Within, "What spiritual quality is being called for in this moment of desperation?", rather than begging and pleading and making deals with God to heal me.

On my third night in the hospital, I became more aware of what was going on around me. The two retired military gentlemen who were sharing the room with me were both suffering from cancer, and I had the uncomfortable opportunity to watch denial operating at its highest level. One of the gentlemen had a hole in his neck to help facilitate breathing instruments that were being put into him. Both of them were smokers and were continuing to smoke in spite of their current difficulties.

The Inner Opening

As I watched the nurses lecture these gentlemen about smoking while being in the hospital, I couldn't help but think about the times I was rushed to the emergency room in the past and promised myself "no more cigarettes." Then after being there for hours getting my lungs opened up, I would have a cigarette as soon as I left the emergency room—just as many of you have made a promise to yourself concerning your addictions to credit card spending, gambling, or overeating, only to return to the scene of the crime time and time again after being given a reprieve.

Watching these gentlemen and myself suffer the way no one should ever have to suffer, the decision to never ever put a cigarette in my mouth again (aided by the gift of desperation and the experience of watching these men give up on life) was truly an answered prayer.

My spiritual resume of a Deeper Love working in my life, time and time again, has given me and others the ability to continue to do the work I do: raising the consciousness of those who have given up on life and who have been hopelessly addicted to life-threatening habits and lifestyles that no longer serve them.

The Conscious Decision

On September 15, 1985, I made the conscious decision to never put another drug or alcoholic drink into my body ever again, no matter what. On September 3, 1986, I made another conscious decision to never put another cigarette into my mouth ever again, no matter what. Both of these decisions (after smoking and using drugs for twenty years, starting at the age of eleven) began to serve as profound catalysts in my life, leading me to accomplish things I never thought I could do.

My yearning to be more connected to this Deeper Love Within—which seemed to do its best work with me while I was laying on my back in my sick bed, but never limited Itself to that circumstance in my life—has now become my greatest asset. In *The Creative Process*, Thomas Troward states, "If you are not conscious of something you are conscious of nothing, and if you are conscious of nothing you are unconscious; so to be conscious at all we must have something to be conscious of."

To make the conscious decision to treat ourselves and others like the offspring of a Power greater than ourselves (which we are intended to be) is to become fully awakened and conscious to the ever-expanding Deeper Love Within. Every so-called crisis we experience in our lives can be flipped into the most profitable episodes of our lives, if we decide to attach a new beneficial meaning to it. In return for this conscious decision to see the lessons and blessings in times of difficulties, we become a beneficial presence on this planet, helping others overcome their difficulties.

In working with those in treatment centers, prisons, hospitals, and individuals over the years, I've seen so many men and woman put down the spoon that would hold their drugs, only to turn around after getting clean and pick up the fork and food that would replace the drugs and alcohol. Oftentimes, just as we would pick up drugs and alcohol to overcome certain feelings and emotions, people with addictive personalities will unknowingly use food much in the same manner.

The disease of addiction manifests itself in many areas of our lives. Even after having many years clean from drugs and alcohol, the addiction can resurface in a new form, such as excessive spending, sex, food, etc.

By making the decision to pray and meditate daily, we don't allow our feelings and emotions to rule our lives. The decision to change our lives—more than we want to stay the same—becomes the catalyst for the ever-expanding good of life to have its way with us. The one thing we have complete control of in our lives is what we make the decision to focus on. Rather than focusing on our defects of the past and fears of the future, we can make the decision to be committed to the infinite possibilities of "now."

As part of the mental conditioning that controls our lives, we have a built-in Universal Support System based in love that can turn around any old thoughts and paradigms that limit us from living life like it is golden. Through the decision to incorporate loving and empowering thoughts and words, we set the framework to live glorious, joyous, and abundant lives.

DAILY · AFFIRMATIONS · OF · TRUTH

POINT OF 6 POWER

DECISIONS

DAY ❶

My decision to love myself and others, no matter what, transcends the meaning of everything that happened to me in the past. *And so it is!*

DAY ❷

My decision to stay in conscious connection to my Higher Power Within is my roadmap to joy, peace, and abundance. *And so it is!*

DAY ❸

My decision to forgive rather than be forgiven, to love rather than be loved allows me to continue to reside in Christ Consciousness. *And so it is!*

DAY 4

Today I am deciding to be the Light of Love that lights up every man and woman I come in contact with. *And so it is!*

DAY 5

My decision not to watch the news today allows me to know that I am in the world but not of the world. *And so it is!*

DAY 6

My decision to begin my day with meditation becomes the starting point for my day to flow with ease and grace. *And so it is!*

DAY 7

My decision to feel and see every so-called setback as a set-up for something greater frees me from fear, worry, and doubt. *And so it is!*

FORGIVENESS

"We make a conscious decision to forgive anyone and everyone who we think may have done us harm, including ourselves; and we take the steps necessary to forgiving them all."

~ POINT OF POWER 7

"Forgiveness is the fragrance that the violet sheds on the heel that has crushed it."

~ MARK TWAIN

Responsibility

Resentments rob us of the benefits and beauty of experiencing the unconditional Deeper Love Within and all of its by-products. If we are to live from the laws of harmony and love, we must first find peace within ourselves and get along with others.

We are not always responsible for what has been done to us by others, but we are always responsible for how we react.

One of the greatest examples of forgiveness was demonstrated by Jesus of Nazareth during his crucifixion when he asked himself and others to "forgive them for they know not what they do." There is a Deeper Love Within each of us that we can draw from to forgive anyone and everyone we perceive as doing us wrong. Unconditional love is that higher aspect of each of us that has never been hurt, harmed, or endangered.

Between 1942 and 1945, Victor Frankl endured four Nazi death camps in which his parents, brother, and pregnant wife disappeared. Because of his unimaginable time in the camps he taught millions of us valuable lessons on how to deal with painful situations while overcoming our own bitterness and resentments. Frankl reminds us in his autobiographical book *Man's Search for Meaning* that "we cannot avoid suffering, but we can choose how we cope with it."

I was dumped by a childhood sweetheart in high school, and as the result of my resentment I set up roadblocks to any women getting close to me at a deeper level for the next fifteen years. Although there were many loving and lovely women in my life, I lacked the spiritual awareness of forgiveness and compassion that would allow me to settle down and get out of my resentments long enough to build anything solid with an equal partner.

It wasn't until some fifteen years later while doing my inner work that I began to attach a new meaning to this episode in my life. I was asked to list all the resentments I had from the time I was in kindergarten, or as far back as I could remember, until the present time. I was also asked to list the names of these people and organizations, and describe how my resentments affected me.

The most surprising part of the questioning was what part I played in these resentments. In being honest and getting out of a victim consciousness, I began to realize that Betty, who was my girlfriend in high school, had every right to dump me based on the truth that I was physically and emotionally unavailable because of my drug addiction.

While this episode with Betty was pretty cut and dried, it was not the case when it came to forgiving Joe. Joe was a friend of the family and no one knew he was a predator and rapist. Joe raped me when I was twelve. The most difficult thing for me was trying to erase this humiliating nightmare out of my memory, and drugs played a major role in doing that. By repressing the feelings associated with the rape, drugs helped me deal with the pain of feeling less than a young man.

In doing this resentment inventory, I began to see how being violated affected me. I believed I could never be a real man unless I killed Joe or made him suffer the way he made me (and most likely others) suffer. I wished the very worst for him. As a member of a gang in Newark, New Jersey, at the age of twelve, I could not tell someone I had been raped by another man and still hope to be seen as tough in the eyes of other gang members (even though I wasn't really tough).

Freedom to Change

Under the loving care of a sponsor and mentor some twenty years later, who guided me through this self-examination process, I began to discuss the fact that Joe had been in and out of penitentiaries most of his life. Possibly, this same cruel and unjust behavior that was imposed on me had probably happened to him as a kid or an adult—and he was doing to others what was done to him.

As I began to attach new meanings to these events of my life, coming from a place of unconditional love and radical forgiveness, they could no longer hold me captive to victimhood. As a result, I began to understand what Victor Frankl was teaching when he said, "It is never the events of our lives that determine our lives, but the inner meaning that we attach to these events that determine our lives."

I began to understand that every mistreatment of another is always a cry for help by the perpetrator. In answering the question of what role did I play in my resentment of Joe raping me, I began to understand that my expectations of Joe were too high, based on where Joe was in consciousness.

This "aha" moment set the stage for me to begin to come from a place of forgiveness and compassion. As the saying goes, if we continue to live with the eye-for-an-eye philosophy, the whole world eventually will go blind.

As I look back, I can tell you that the things I benefited from the most from in this recovery process were usually the things I didn't want to do. Nowhere in my fear-based upbringing would I ever have conceived of myself as being able to forgive anyone for this heinous crime or injustice toward me. This kind of forgiveness is what I now understand as coming from a Deeper Love Within.

Blame Throwers

My mother played a major role in this forgiving process as well. When I was thirteen, I was sent to a state home for boys in Jamesburg, New Jersey. My sentence was nine months for a combination of petty crimes. Before going to this detention center, my mother often warned me that if I ever went to jail (following in my older brother's footsteps), I could count on her not taking time out of her busy work schedule to come visit me.

When this promise actually turned into a reality, I was left feeling abandoned and unloved. My long list of long-lasting resentments was now in full effect. It wasn't until I began to examine the exact nature of these defects showing up in the area of resentments that I began wanting to understand rather than wanting to be understood.

My grandmother was an alcoholic many years ago, and in those days, chronic alcoholics were put into mental institutions. (By the way, alcoholics and addicts are still put into mental institutions, they are just cleverly disguised as treatment centers and prisons.) When she was committed to a mental institution, my mother was forced to live with two aunts who unwillingly took on the task of raising her. This unwillingness was no secret to my mother. As a matter fact, she was emotionally and physically abused in this process.

Oftentimes, people who come from an abusive upbringing confuse this abuse with tough love, and they unconsciously pass this abuse on as tough love to others. This was my mother's case in passing it on to her children. Emotional abuse can be just as damaging as physical abuse. Growing up in a household where words of encouragement and feelings of love were never expressed or mentioned, coupled with occasional ass whippings, left me never wanting to be at home. As a result, I spent as little time there as I could while growing up.

It wasn't until years later that I began to understand the

statement from Narcotics Anonymous, "It is through our inability to accept personal responsibility that we create our own problems." Through the loving process of coming to understand others, rather than wanting to be understood, I began to see my mother through the eyes of a Deeper Love Within. I began to understand that my mother did the very best she could with what she had to work with (her state of consciousness).

When I consider all that she went through in her life, and recognizing that she still had the courage to stick it out and raise six children, she is now my hero.

The process of self-discovery and self-acceptance forces us to put away our blame throwers and to see the light instead of the shadows in all situations. To forgive others and ourselves for holding contempt, we in turn open the inner eye to see the best in others and in ourselves.

Self-Forgiveness

When we begin to live life from this higher spiritual consciousness, we open ourselves up to understanding rather than always wanting to be understood. As students of truth on the path to spiritual liberation, we have a responsibility to see the face of a Deeper Love in everyone we meet, in spite of their fear-based actions. As spiritual ambassadors of unconditional love, we can create from a place of love rather than reacting from a place of fear.

As spiritual beings grounded in the absolute truth of our divinity rather than our depravity, we become the examples of the Unconditional Love we want to see in the world.

The biggest payoff of forgiveness is self-forgiveness, more so than forgiving others. We can begin the process by forgiving ourselves for holding onto any erroneous thoughts of others based on their fear-based actions. When we are not coming from a place of unconditional love, it's because we are under the illusion that we are going to lose something we have or not get something we want.

Ralph Waldo Emerson, writing about Jesus, said, "His heart was as great as the world, but there was no room to hold the memory of wrong."

Love Thyself

"You are my beloved child with whom I am well pleased" (Mark 1:11). I was always unknowingly seeking the love and approval of my mother through other people and other things—until a major breakthrough came my way.

After walking away from my award-winning restaurant, my wife, and everything that gave my life so-called meaning at the time, I sank into a depression. I was going through a divorce and a bankruptcy, both financial and spiritual. I had been clean for nineteen years, and I knew drugs and alcohol were not the solution to my problems at this point in my recovery process.

I entered therapy and began to heal my wounded child within. I was directed to come home after work and, before turning on the music or television, have a seat on the sofa with no distractions from the phone, books, or anything else. I was to then find a photo of me as a child when I was at my youngest and most innocent state—and with this photo in hand, to close my eyes and continue to see this child.

For seven days I practiced visioning this innocent child sitting on my lap as part of me. I began to hug myself, thus hugging the younger innocent me. While hugging myself and my inner child, I began to tell this child, "I love you and I will always be there for you." I went on to tell my inner child, "You are a very special part of me, and I will never leave or forsake you." I continued telling my inner child everything a loving and present parent would say, free of guilt and shame, to help him feel loved and comforted.

This process was another one of the biggest breakthroughs in my inner healing. There is an inner child within each of us who needs our love. And the love your inner child is seeking is seeking you. This is the kind of big boy and big girl stuff that is needed in the process of healing and getting out of victim mode.

After unknowingly letting the actions of others determine my self-worth for so long, I decided that instead of trying to change the people I had perceived as doing me harm, I would instead work on changing my thoughts and feelings about those people—and about myself.

7—FORGIVENESS

We all have made mistakes in our lives, but those of us who have made the decision to continue to grow and develop can't waste our precious time feeling sorry for ourselves or harboring resentments. From this state of awareness and consciousness we come to know that the love and forgiveness we are seeking is also seeking us. It is the Deeper Love Within that has always been there, waiting to have Its way with us, no matter what.

DAILY · AFFIRMATIONS · OF · TRUTH

POINT OF **7** POWER

FORGIVENESS

DAY ❶

My Deeper Love Within can never forgive me for it has never condemned me. I am the activity of this Deeper Love, in which It is well pleased. *And so it is!*

DAY ❷

I forgive myself for all the missteps I have taken in life, knowing that these steps have led me to loving myself unconditionally. *And so it is!*

DAY ❸

It is from the Christ Consciousness that dwells within me that I forgive others, for they know not what they do. *And so it is!*

DAY ❹

By making the decision to forgive others, I begin to see their eternal light shining in them, instead of a lampshade. *And so it is!*

DAY 5

As part of the infinite power of Unconditional Love that loves us no matter what, I say "yes" to forgiving myself and others. *And so it is!*

DAY 6

I forgive you today, because my peace of mind depends on it. *And so it is!*

DAY 7

In knowing that Love loves to love, I forgive myself for anything that has stood in the way of me being my very best. *And so it is!*

CHAPTER 8

UNCONDITIONAL LOVE

"We now make a commitment to hold everyone, including ourselves, in the highest state of consciousness by practicing unconditional love everywhere we go."

~ POINT OF POWER 8

"To grow in unconditional love and in beauty is spirituality."

~GURUDEV SRI SRI RAVI SHANKAR

Love Loves to Love

There is within each of us a deep yearning to love and be loved. Unlike some animals that are taught to fend for themselves the day they are born, we depend on the love of each other for our survival. Until we find the inner strength to know ourselves at a deeper level, we project onto others exactly what was projected onto us, following someone else's example to model this thing we call love. At any given time, we can make the decision not to love this or that or him or her. But because Love loves to love, we get the chance to see the best in—and to want the best for—everyone we come in contact with. This is the starting point in activating the principle and gift of Love.

In speaking with thousands of people in this recovery process over the years, I've observed and experienced in my own evolution that the last thing we seem to be able to grasp in this journey of spiritual growth and development is the ability to love ourselves. Coming from a less-than-nurturing household can make the task seem more challenging, to say the least, but not impossible.

The great American self-help author and motivational speaker Wayne Dyer, who spent much of his adolescence in an orphanage on the east side of Detroit, went on to become a powerful example of one who practiced unconditional love in all his affairs, despite his surroundings when he was growing up. Dyer always knew that regardless of his external environment and circumstances, there was a power greater than his surroundings, working on his behalf and on the behalf of all mankind.

The Intention to Love

Early on in my recovery process there were people who loved me until I could love myself. We begin the practice of self-love the day we make the commitment to no longer put drugs, alcohol, cigarettes, unhealthy foods, or unloving thoughts into our bodies and minds. Instead, we choose to balance, cleanse, and nurture every cell, organ, action, and function of our bodies and minds.

In attending twelve-step meetings early in my recovery, I met all kinds of people with crazy and funny personalities from different walks of life. The common denominator was that we were all (for the most part) trying to stay clean, and in our times of differences, we learned to place the principles of love for each other over our personalities.

If we see and want the very best for everyone we come into contact with (including our so-called enemies) while going about our daily business, it would be impossible for us not to have love, peace, and joy break out at every corner we turn.

8—UNCONDITIONAL LOVE

We also can decide at any time to let go of any self-defeating beliefs we have about life that keep us stagnant in our spiritual growth and development. No healing can take place in our body, or our body of affairs, without an intention to treat ourselves like the kings and queens we are intended to be.

All loving intentions backed and supported by universal love open up our hearts and activate our recovery process. The biggest breakthroughs in our lives, when it comes to love, will come as a result of our commitment to forgiving ourselves and others whom we perceive as having done us wrong.

Nelson Mandela had every excuse to give up on South Africa —and to be bitter and resentful after being imprisoned for twenty-seven years. Because he knew and practiced unconditional love, he made it possible for millions who have read his story to practice compassion, forgiveness, and unconditional love. He said, "As I walked out the door toward the gate that would lead to my freedom, I knew that if I didn't leave my bitterness and hatred behind, I'd still be in prison."

People make mistakes and are not always drawing from that divine and perfect pattern within themselves. But unconditional love is always perfect, and its practice allows us to see beyond the mistakes of ourselves and others, so Love will have Its way with us.

While working in Donovan State Prison in San Diego some years ago, after taking a break from the food service business and working as a drug and alcohol counselor, I had an inmate client who was extremely angry and totally unconscious of his habit of blaming everyone else for his constant cycle of being in and out of jail. While being verbally and physically abused by his father played a large role in his angry traits from time to time, this past abuse was in no way a life sentence or cop-out for him to give up on life.

His brother, who was a well-to-do attorney in San Diego, showed up to visit one day. We had the opportunity to speak later, and during our conversation I noticed how different the brothers were, specifically concerning their outlooks on life. I said, "If you don't mind me asking, how is it that you two brothers could come from the same father and the same household, and yet are so different?" He explained to me that he had set an intention to never ever be like his father and, more importantly, to forgive his father.

I feel that Ella Wheeler Wilcox sums up this scenario best:

> *But to every man there openeth,*
> *A high way and a low,*
> *And every mind decideth,*
> *The way his soul shall go.*
> *One ship sails East,*
> *And another West,*
> *By the self-same winds that blow,*
> *'Tis the set of the sails*
> *And not the gales,*
> *That tells the way we go.*

Later, my client and I discussed the importance of taking 100 percent responsibility for his life and getting out of his victim mode of thinking. We talked about using his brother and so many others who were abused even more than he was as examples to overcoming his obstacles. By taking 100 percent responsibility for his life, he began to turn his life around.

Whether we are serving time physically or locked in the prison of our own minds, we are always free to participate in a process of inner transformation and renewal. By turning the key of a Deeper Love Within, we begin to unlock our love for others and our own situations. This self-contemplation breaks down our wall of resentments (or any other seeming roadblocks that would stand in our way), and enables us to become living examples of unconditional love.

Our commitment and intention to be a beneficial presence on this planet—preceded by a spiritual awakening—will eventually bring us to a burning desire to raise the consciousness of others who have suffered at the hands of addiction or any other felt sense of separation from this Deeper Love Within. As spiritual practitioners (those who are practicing spiritual principles) and metaphysicians (those who are practicing metaphysical principles), we have the responsibility to see the "All-ness" of love, peace, spirit, and power in everyone we encounter throughout the course our day.

We are to be grounded in the absolute truth that we live in a universe built on love. It is in our spiritual DNA to be the love that others are seeking, to tap into the truth that we are in essence and substance pure love, beauty, and intelligence. Our quest is not to get love but to seek opportunities to let this pure love flow from us. And in return, we become a magnet for the Love of Life.

DAILY · AFFIRMATIONS · OF · TRUTH

POINT OF **8** *POWER*

UNCONDITIONAL LOVE

DAY 1

There is a Universal Love guiding me everywhere I go. The love I have been seeking is seeking me. In love I live, move, and have my being. *And so it is!*

DAY 2

Today I allow this Universal Love to guide me in every decision I make. With Universal Love as my guide, I shall never be lost. *And so it is!*

DAY 3

The Divine Source of my life provides me with everything I need. With this Deeper Love as my Shepherd, I shall not want. *And so it is!*

POINT OF 8 POWER

DAY 4

Knowing that I reap what I sow, I plant seeds of love in my subconscious mind and watch love break out everywhere I go. *And so it is!*

DAY 5

I say "yes" to that Deeper Love Within me. It shows up pouring Itself out stupendously in all my affairs. *And so it is!*

DAY 6

Today I commit to the Unconditional Love of Life. I see the very best in everyone I meet and in every situation I encounter. *And so it is!*

DAY 7

As I continue to plant seed thoughts of love, I am guaranteed to continue to live from the Overflow of Love. *And so it is!*

CHAPTER 9

GRATEFULNESS

"We commit to writing a gratitude list, thus allowing ourselves to maintain a daily attitude of gratitude."

~ POINT OF POWER 9

"The enlightened give thanks for what most people take for granted. As you begin to be grateful for what most people take for granted, the vibration of gratitude makes you more receptive to good in your life."

~ MICHAEL BERNARD BECKWITH

Lessons and Blessings

In 1971, as a high school kid in East Orange, New Jersey, I joined the Nation of Islam. Many of my friends in Newark and East Orange were joining as a show of social consciousness, and in my senior year, my close friend and I were approached by an older guy who represented a new order of Islam. He hoped to recruit us. He managed to recruit my friend, but something never felt right about this new order for me. Some months later, my friend and this older man were found in a park in Newark, dead and beheaded. Some say it was in retaliation and connection to the murder of Minister James Shabazz of Mosque 25 in Newark.

I also had a close friend in high school named Lee, who went on a murdering rampage and wound up serving a triple life sentence in Rahway State Prison at the age of nineteen.

Then there was Paul, another dear friend. One morning, we crossed paths while we were each on our way to different high schools. Paul suggested that we both play hooky (skip school). On any other day, this suggestion would have been music to my ears. But on this particular morning, I decided I would go to school. After school that day, I was walking down the street where Paul lived, when his brother Alex ran up to me and told me Paul was in trouble. Upon entering Paul's bedroom, I sadly saw Paul laying on a urine-soaked mattress, convulsing from the nose and mouth as a result of an overdose of barbiturates. By the time the paramedics came, it was too late. Paul died at the age of seventeen.

When I arrived at Miramar Naval Air Station in California for drug rehabilitation in 1985, I was asked to write about everything in my life I was grateful for, in an attempt to make me aware of what was working in my life (instead of focusing on my failures). I began to write about these three friends, and so many more experiences, where I managed to avoid death, long prison terms, and mental illness. (Some might question whether I really avoided the mental illness aspect, based on some of my decisions.)

I lost many friends and family members who were involved in the same day-to-day madness I was involved in, but here I was alive—and I was being given the opportunity to see these experiences as vital gifts in leading me to the next stage of my spiritual growth and development.

With all I saw and experienced in the first thirty-one years of my life, I felt wonderfully grateful for the lessons and blessings that set the stage for my passion for living and turning my life around, that I now experience today.

In looking back at all of my near-death experiences and difficulties I have faced in my life, I came to the realization that they were great ammunition for helping others walk through their problems in life. In working with those who have given up on their dreams and aspirations, my responsibility as a metaphysician and recovery coach is to constantly remind myself and others that life has never given up on us. No matter how many times we have been down, life is always for us and never against us. Life and all of its infinite wonders stand at the door of our soul, waiting to express themselves in all of our affairs.

An Opening for the Gifts

Based on my experience and the experience of others I have worked with on this spiritual path, I believe a grateful recovering person will never go back to their old lifestyle. A mind singularly focused on gratitude becomes the engine for living life with a sense of renewal and purpose.

In becoming conscious of the responsibility each of us bears to those who will come behind us into this process of recovery, no matter what they may be recovering from, gratitude becomes essential for everything meaningful we shall accomplish in our lives. No matter the difficulties we may have bumped up against, we can rest assured that if our concepts of those events were different—based in an attitude of gratitude—we would see those events as blessings in disguise. Standing firm in the belief that there is a Perfect Power within each of us, more powerful than any obstacle we may come up against, allows us to continue to move through our day with ease and grace.

There was a time early in my recovery when I would fall into a funk and start complaining to my sponsor (recovery coach) about the things that weren't working in my life. He would invite me out to lunch or dinner, and it would usually be somewhere near skid row (or at least San Diego's version of skid row). He would park the car a long distance from where we were to actually eat and make a point to stop occasionally along the way while walking, cleverly tying his shoe or sitting down for a minute whenever we got close to someone who was homeless. This experience of seeing homeless people who had so much less in their lives really began to put my problems into perspective. I eventually caught onto his ploy, but it worked.

The Practice

If there is ever a time when I'm unhappy with my life, I can always choose to focus on the 90 percent of things that are working, thus giving less attention to the 10 percent of things that are not working. In doing this, the 10 percent of things that are not working will have no credence. It takes only a split second to think of our Deeper Love Within that is bringing forth more of what we are putting our attention on.

Here is a practice I always recommend to those I work with: When life seems too much to bear, write down twenty-five things you are grateful for just before going to bed each night. In this process of writing about the things and people that you are grateful for, you begin to impregnate your subconscious mind with a brighter and more uplifting view of life. As you become more relaxed, the conscious thoughts of those things you worried about will slowly move out of the way, and feelings of gratitude will become a larger part of your life. Upon waking up in the morning with a feeling of rejuvenation, read over your gratitude list to begin your day. This process should be repeated for at least seven days—more if needed.

As long as we imagine our so-called problems as our only reality, we cut ourselves off from the many blessings and gifts waiting to be experienced from the overflow of love, beauty, and abundance. However, when we view things from the mountaintop of life, and see things from this higher state of consciousness, we soon discover that all is well.

DAILY · AFFIRMATIONS · OF · TRUTH

POINT OF ❾ POWER

GRATEFULNESS

DAY ❶

I nourish my thoughts today with the warmth of gratitude and thanksgiving, knowing all of my needs are met. *And so it is!*

DAY ❷

Opportunities await my acceptance everywhere I go—and gratitude wells up in me with every breath I breathe. *And so it is!*

DAY ❸

In a constant state of gratitude for all the blessings that are coming my way moment by moment, I am ready to receive even more than I can imagine. *And so it is!*

DAY ❹

With an attitude of gratitude, I set the stage for my life to unfold in a most magnificent way. *And so it is!*

DAY 5

My gratitude speaks through me in the sacred service I provide for others on their path in life. My life is a life of giving. *And so it is!*

DAY 6

In waking up this morning full to overflowing with gratitude. I deeply feel and experience the love of life. *And so it is!*

DAY 7

I give praise and gratitude for all of the so-called difficulties in my life, knowing they are simply lessons and blessings in disguise. *And so it is!*

MINDFUL MEDITATION

*"We dedicate ourselves to the daily practice
of meditation for the sole purpose of anchoring ourselves
in heaven, right here on Earth."*

~ POINT OF POWER 10

*"If you are depressed,
you are living in the past. If you are anxious,
you are living in the future. If you are at peace,
you are living in the present."*

~ SOURCE UNKNOWN

Be Still and Know that I Am

When we come into the awareness that I Am Love, I Am Peace, I Am Life and Intelligence, we set the foundation to see ourselves as the Universe sees us—as Its own manifestation, in which It is well pleased.

"Be ye therefore perfect, even as your Father who is in heaven is perfect" (Matthew 5:48). If the Kingdom of God's presence lies within us (as most spiritual teachings have taught us), there also lies within a Divine and Perfect Pattern in which we can extract everything we need to have life, and to have it peacefully and abundantly.

An Inside Job

In *Walden*, Henry David Thoreau wrote, "Most of the luxuries, and many of the so-called comforts of life, are not only indispensable, but positive hindrances to the elevation of mankind."

After being clean for nineteen years, I was sitting in the office of Sherman's Cajun and Creole Buffet in San Diego, counting the proceeds from a financially prosperous day. Suddenly, a question came to me: Is this all there is to life?

This question set into motion a transformational turn in my life that I never saw coming. You see, I had always been taught to believe that life was an indigenous process—meaning that the more I accumulated, the better off I would be. I was never taught the lesson of Matthew 6:33: "Seek ye first the kingdom of God and all else shall be added." That kingdom, as I understand it today, is my conscious connection to the kingdom of God within me, an endogenous process.

For the next year I began to painfully walk away from everything I thought defined me: the business, the marriage, the house, and the cars. Don't get me wrong. It's perfectly fine to have these things in our lives as long as they don't define us. It turned out that the thing missing from my life was the burning desire to know myself at a deeper level through a conscious connection to my Higher Power within. This burning desire came with a price tag, sometimes described as the dark night of the soul.

At that point in my life, I had a fixed belief that things were supposed to go a certain way—and when those things didn't go a certain way according to my best laid plans, depression set in (whether it be mild or major).

For the next two years, the letting go of my business, marriage, house, and cars came at a heavy price. I had to pay spousal support, I owed the government more than thirty-three thousand dollars, and my credit was shot as I went through a major bankruptcy. Most of all, the feeling that I had failed as a father, a business owner, a mentor, and a husband all weighed heavily on me.

Know Thyself

As I sat one morning at a coffee shop, I began to contemplate suicide for the first time in my life. Someone lovingly and jokingly reminded me that if I killed myself, I would be killing the wrong guy. Thankfully, my sponsor and the people who loved and supported me knew there was a Power within me that was greater than the sense of separation I was experiencing.

I am also grateful for the guys I was sponsoring during that time, who in turn unknowingly began to sponsor *me* through this difficult period in my life. Today, I believe there is a Power and Love within each of us that is greater than any obstacle that will ever come our way.

During this time, I was visiting a used bookstore, and a book on the metaphysical teachings of the great master teachers fell into my hands. After reading this book (and many more), I began to open my inner eye and heart to what all of the spiritual masters had been teaching: The spiritual qualities of life are our divine birthright, waiting to give birth through our higher states of consciousness.

After walking away from my restaurant that was bringing in close to $1 million dollars a year, I went to work in a prison as a drug counselor making eleven dollars an hour as a way of trying to find myself and the deeper meaning of life. After going to work for this new company for six months, I realized this position was not going to be enough to pay my bills. Rather than allowing me walk away, the company offered to give me a new position (with a huge pay raise) and relocate me from San Diego to Los Angeles. This new position involved counseling and teaching cooking to men who were coming out of prison.

In Los Angeles, I began a deeper meditation practice that allowed me to be at peace even in the most difficult times—independent of the fear, worry, and doubt that often plagued me during my times of depression.

There was a rose garden next to the University of Southern California, a five-minute walk from this new job, where I would go every morning before work (and sometimes during my lunch break). In the mornings I would hop the fence, since I often got to the rose garden before the gate was opened to the public. During these walking and sitting meditations, I was surrounded by more than one hundred types of roses, in a garden the size of a football field.

I had never felt a sense of peace like the kind I felt while in this garden of nature with all of its beauty. It was during these times of being consciously connected to a Deeper Love Within that I came to believe that everything I needed was inside of me, and that wherever I Am, God is, waiting to express Itself as Eternal Peace through me.

I learned to be like the lilies of the field that never doubted or worried about how they were to survive. In this meditative silence I began to realize that all of my needs were met. Since that time, meditation has become the most important aspect of my life.

When I set the intention to focus on my breath, and not on my thinking, I am connected to a Deeper Love Within. In this stillness, I came to know that "I Am that Thou art and Thou art that I Am." While meditating in the silence, I also came to know that outside of my thinking there are no problems in life. Meditation allows us the opportunity to be mindful of our thinking, without being ruled by it or judging it. We think—but we are so much more than what we think.

It's been said that life is a series of events passing through our lives in which we get to experience those events without being attached. All suffering comes as a result of our attachment to these events. Meditation allows each of us the quiet time to practice non-attachment to events of the past and fears of the future.

Within each of us lies the undiscovered possibility of perfect peace, the peace beyond all human understanding. We are here to have it, and have it abundantly, with no conditions. We give birth to these undiscovered possibilities by resting in the awareness and consciousness that "I and the Father/Mother God Presence are One."

I'm not one of those people who has a "burning bush" meditation experience very often (although I have had a few similar experiences). But what I can tell you is that every time I meditate, I experience a sense of peace and calmness that follows me throughout my day. Money, drugs, and sex could never buy this Inner Knowing, which tells me that I'm loved and constantly protected. There are days when I can stand in grocery lines or sit in a traffic jam in my car and still experience great "aha" moments outside of my thinking—and often in spite of my thinking.

We owe it to ourselves to set aside a minimum of fifteen minutes twice a day to rest in this conscious awareness and connection to this truth. Wherever we are, Spirit must be in its fullness—there is no spot where Spirit is not. Our lives are the out-picturing of this great force field of love, beauty, and intelligence.

I've often been reminded that our greatest problems in life have come as result of our felt sense of separation from our oneness with the All-ness of this Infinite and Eternal Power, Presence, and Deeper Love Within. There's something to be said about the person who takes time out of their busy daily schedule to walk through a park, sit on a beach, or go on a hike —detaching themselves from the hustle and bustle of the world in order to practice the Presence of this Living Power and Peace Within, which is much greater than the world. We are then "in the world but not of the world."

As one who likes walking meditations, oftentimes through walking trails, parks, and mountains, I always set the intention to act as if it is my first time going through these trails, even if I have been there before. In doing so, I am able to be present and in awe of the many wonders that surround me.

DAILY · AFFIRMATIONS · OF · TRUTH

POINT OF 10 POWER

MINDFUL MEDITATION

DAY 1

I have a conscious connection with the great I Am Presence and rest in the awareness that my life is in divine and perfect order. *And so it is!*

DAY 2

I am so grateful to be in that gap between thoughts during the silence and to experience Almighty Joy. *And so it is!*

DAY 3

With mindful meditation I open the door to the Peace That Passes All Understanding. *And so it is!*

DAY 4

Through my commitment to daily meditation, my awareness

POINT OF 10 POWER

of the Presence of a Deeper Love Within grows stronger every day. *And so it is!*

DAY 5

Meditation constantly reveals the higher aspect of me within, which has never been hurt, harmed, or endangered. *And so it is!*

DAY 6

In meditation, I turn to that "Secret Place of the Most-High," and I discover the "Kingdom of God is at hand." *And so it is!*

DAY 7

Just for today, through soft inner listening in the silence of meditation, I'm assured that my life is in divine and perfect order. *And so it is!*

CHAPTER 11

CREATIVE VISUALIZATION

*"Through the process of creative visualization,
we begin to live our lives from the overflow of life."*

~ POINT OF POWER 11

*"Whatever the mind can conceive and believe,
the mind can achieve."*

~ NAPOLEON HILL

11 — CREATIVE VISUALIZATION

Believing Is Seeing

Early in my recovery, I was about to purchase my first home in San Diego. I met with a good friend who was a real estate agent in La Jolla, California. After having lunch, he drove me to see a house he had just sold overlooking the beach. Out of a consciousness of lack and limitation I said, "I can't even imagine living in a house so big and beautiful." His reply was, "And you won't live in a place so big and so beautiful, if you can't imagine it." He said it so nonchalantly, as if he already knew about the law of attraction that I had yet to learn about.

Every major breakthrough in my life, which in most cases have come after a breakdown, were the result of me giving up my assumption that the way I see things from a human point of view is the way things really are or should be. When I'm coming from this limited point of view, I'm failing to realize that "eyes have not seen, nor ears heard" what the Universe has in store for me.

When I came to Los Angeles to work as a chef and substance abuse counselor, I was the only twelve-step staff member. During that time, numerous clients were directed to twelve-step meetings as part of their parole and probation with the court system. I was given the task and opportunity to give seminars every Friday night, breaking down the twelve steps of recovery to one hundred or more of these clients.

As I began to get more and more into a metaphysical way of seeing myself and life from a higher state of consciousness, I began to experience a divine discontent and inner conflict with myself and what I was teaching. I could no longer in good conscience identify with the many negative and limiting labels we put on ourselves as recovering addicts and alcoholics. As a result of trying to teach what I could no longer adhere to, I began to unconsciously choke myself off from a greater truth that was trying to reveal itself through me.

The Revelation

This divine discontent would lead me to the last asthma attack I would have. I was hospitalized in the intensive care unit, and for three of the eight days I was there, my attack was so severe they intubated me. During this time, I felt like I was having an out-of-body experience—like the "old Sherman" with all of his fears, worries, and doubts had died. I was being lifted in Spirit from my old body lying in the hospital bed into to a vibrant and spiritually awakened "new Sherman," without a care in the world.

Immediately after this spiritual experience, my lungs began to miraculously open, along with my heart. I started having great insights and revelations. I began having visions of myself teaching this new metaphysical approach to recovery, based on the twelve points of power, in several locations each week, even using PowerPoint presentations (although I had no experience with PowerPoint). I would not see any visitors or receive any phone calls in order to remain in this blissful state.

Upon leaving the hospital, I met with the director of operations of the treatment center where I worked to inform him that I could no longer do seminars based on the old information and formats I had been teaching.

Through meditation and the process of creative visualization, the spiritual revelation I experienced allowed me to see life's bigger plan for me. Life is always trying to reveal Its greater loving plan for us, although most of us cannot accept these plans.

For the next ten years, I began to use every opportunity I had to express and talk about this Deeper Love Within. Every Friday night, I would speak to a group of 150 men. Every Tuesday night, I would speak to twenty-five disabled veterans. I also facilitated book studies in San Diego and Los Angeles, as well as facilitating Toastmaster meetings every Saturday morning.

The Inner Vision

Creative visualization allows us to express the inner visions constantly being revealed to us as our greatest yet-to-be. In this process, we let go of the question that asks how we are to do what has been revealed to us in those quiet moments—instead focusing on the what and the why. The how will be always revealed.

It's been said that the greatest fear in life, second only to death, is public speaking. As a kid in grammar school, I would often sit behind the biggest kids in class to shield and hide myself from the teacher, praying to God the teacher would not call on me to talk or answer a question. This self-centered fear was the downfall for a large part of my life and can still be if I'm not consciously connected to my Deeper Love Within. As a result of turning my will and my life over to the care of this Deeper Love Within, the fear of speaking no longer paralyzes me.

I discovered that I had been using creative visualization all my life but was totally unaware of it. When we get an idea from Universal Intelligence (which is the Intelligence behind all ideas) and we began to embrace the idea, feel the idea, and see the idea as reality, the idea is then brought into manifestation. Unfortunately, many of us use creative visualization to bring into manifestation what we don't want instead of what we do want. Some people want to argue vehemently about what's wrong with the world instead of being grateful for life's many wonders— and as a result, life will give them more of what's wrong, as part of their unconscious co-creation.

Life will always give us more of whatever exists where we place our co-creative energy. There is an infinite field of love, beauty and intelligence that will support our inner visions. When we have visions of love backed by feelings of love, rather than fear, as our starting point in consciousness, all things *are* possible. Indeed, all things are possible to those who believe and feel they are possible.

How do you know the difference between vision and ego?
1. When a vision comes to you, ask yourself how the world

benefits by this vision. In this asking, you will know if it is coming from a place of fear or love.
2. After asking this question, begin to write down the many ways that the world will benefit from this vision.
3. Ask yourself, "What talents and gifts do I possess that can be used in bringing this vision into manifestation?" Then ask, "What talents and gifts can I improve upon?"
4. Take three actions that will lead you closer to that vision becoming a goal.
5. Make sure you continue your meditation and affirmative prayers, speaking the word of truth, geared in the direction of this vision.

Each of us has the ability to visualize success and make our dreams become our reality by taking the time to listen to our inner promptings, followed by the necessary footwork. To let our setbacks of yesterday or our fears of tomorrow stop us from visioning beyond our current situation and circumstances is to become prisoners of our own minds.

The clearer we are about our God qualities and the ways in which we can express them, the more our visions will be revealed to us, including the details of what it would look and feel like to activate our gifts and talents within the world.

Having had a spiritual awakening through this process of setting spiritual goals and intentions, all directed to a conscious connection with a Deeper Love Within, I became conscious to the truth that there is no higher purpose in our lives than to be of service to others.

DAILY · AFFIRMATIONS · OF · TRUTH

POINT OF 11 POWER

CREATIVE VISUALIZATION

DAY 1

It is from the greatest vision of the grandest version of myself that my life continues to unfold in a most magnificent way. *And so it is!*

DAY 2

With my eternal vision from the overflow of an ocean of abundance and prosperity, I claim that all of my needs are met. *And so it is!*

DAY 3

The light of God shines Its eternal vision of love through me. I brightly shine this inner light on everyone I meet. *And so it is!*

DAY ❹

Visions of perfect health and wholeness rejuvenate and regenerate every cell in my body. *And so it is!*

DAY ❺

Through the process of creative visualization, I allow the mighty I Am Presence to become my roadmap for my life. *And so it is!*

DAY ❻

Creative visualization activates the principle of abundance, reminding me that life is pouring its blessings out to me forever. *And so it is!*

DAY ❼

There is an Infinite Power and Presence within me that reveals Itself through creative visualization. I say "yes" to this creative process of life. *And so it is!*

CHAPTER 12

GIVING BACK

*"As spiritual ambassadors of Love
and Light, we accept our responsibility to go forth
and multiply this consciousness."*

~ POINT OF POWER 12

*"Today I will give others only the gifts that
I want to accept for myself."*

~ GERALD G. JAMPOLSKY

Courage to Change

As I've recounted in this book, I was deeply involved in gang activity as a kid growing up in Newark. In the summertime, I would sit with my friends on the corner, waiting for delivery trucks to deliver their supplies to Freddie's Grocery Store. While the delivery men were inside, we would systematically, with strategic lookouts in place, begin to unload the truck's goods without consent of the owner. It didn't matter whether it was a soda truck, a pastry truck, a fruit truck, or general groceries, everything was fair game for our stealing. Dishonesty had become a way of life.

We in large part resembled "The East Side Kids" or "The Bowery Boys" (a show about young thugs from New York City's East Side in the 1950s). These were the kind of activities that began to mold my life at the early age of ten years old. It became my responsibility to steal your stuff and then help you look for it, in an attempt to have you believe that I had nothing to do with it.

We would often go to richer neighborhoods with the mentality that as long as we were stealing from the wealthy and not the poor, we could justify our behavior—sort of a Robin Hood mentality. As a kid I thought it took a lot of courage to climb through people's windows when no one was at home or to pull a gun or a knife on someone.

Through my willingness to change more than I wanted to stay the same, I learned the difference between courage and insanity.

When I began my recovery process in 1985, the Universe brought a mentor into my life who would be one of the living examples I needed to change my distorted views. Although much had changed from those days of hanging out on the corner and robbing delivery trucks, there was still a deep-rooted dishonesty, based in fear, that had not changed yet.

My mentor (who grew up in Spanish Harlem, New York) taught me what it meant to be a man of integrity through his living examples and the examples of so many others who had changed their lives. He ingrained in me the belief that the only thing that needed to be changed within me was—everything. I watched men and woman much like me—who came from the ghetto's broken homes and abusive upbringings, with extremely limited views and consciousnesses—become some of the biggest spiritual role models of my life.

I knew deep within that if I maintained a burning desire to stay clean, coupled with the willingness to change more than I wanted to stay the same, I, too, could someday be a role model for someone else in life. As much as I paid close attention to those who taught me to steal, lie, and cheat growing up, I began to pay just as much attention (and even more) to those who were now teaching me how to stop lying, stealing, and using drugs and alcohol.

In Service to Others

It is my belief—based on my own actual experience and the experiences of others who have come from dark backgrounds—that it can only be an act of providence combined with the willingness to change that will turn around the life of someone like me. As someone whose life was rooted in self-centered fear and low self-esteem, I soon learned that the most estimable thing I could do to begin feeling like a part of humanity was to be of service to someone else without expecting anything in return.

Early on in my recovery, I began to experience feelings of being a part of something much greater than my little self, through the service commitments that I had begun to take on. With so many people suffering from addictions of some sort, I began to feel a sense of overwhelming gratitude. These feelings would often bring me to tears—more importantly, tears of joy.

Some of my greatest feelings of purpose and meaning came from volunteering in jails and institutions where I would talk to the incarcerated men and women and share my experiences in overcoming my own addictive patterns in life. I would have the joy of seeing some of these men or women years later, and they would remind me of the time I came to see them in jail or their treatment center and planted the seed of hope in their hearts and subconscious minds, that recovery from this devastating disease of addiction was possible.

I will forever be indebted to the recovery community for as long as I live, move, and have my being. It is with great privilege and joy that I do whatever I can to be of service to someone else who has lost their way in life. We are not here to live our lives solely for ourselves but to become a beneficial presence on this planet for everyone.

There is a higher state of being within us that beckons us to give even when we think we have nothing to give—and to love even when we think we have no love.

Our task is to say "yes" to our great opportunities to be of service in the world. And when we expand our willingness, the Universe will always respond to our spiritual "yes." The many gifts I receive in life will always be in direct proportion to the service I provide to others. The Universe is constantly seeking to express Itself through us—and it seeks the best channel whereby It can do the most good. All we have to do is say, "Show me the way," and let God be God in us, through us, and as us.

Life is a precious gift that invites each of us to give more, do more, and be more (and never less) than our greatest yet-to-be. I found that when I began to do more than what was expected of me at work, and when I loved more unconditionally at home, I started to become more thoughtful and kinder, even in California traffic. I became a joyous giver and receiver in my spiritual community, and my life began to take on a new meaning.

And this transformation came from a guy who once thought it was his obligation to steal your stuff, and then help you look for it.

Those who are involved in the spiritual practice of life on Life's terms, will continue to evolve into something much greater than they could imagine. An act of kindness, an hour or two of service to others, a heartfelt "amend" to someone—these are but a few of the new states of awareness that we get to exude throughout the course of our day, as we connect to our Higher State of Being.

DAILY · AFFIRMATIONS · OF · TRUTH

POINT OF  POWER

GIVING BACK

DAY 1

As a spiritual vessel for the Love of Life, I give back freely through my God-given talents what was so lovingly given to me. *And so it is!*

DAY 2

Knowing that Love loves to love, I say "yes" to being a vehicle of Love, which expresses Itself each and every day through me. *And so it is!*

DAY 3

Radiant ecstasy and bliss continually show up as the "I Am" Presence within me. I share this ecstasy and bliss with the world. *And so it is!*

DAY 4

From within a state of peace, I dwell in the Secret Place of the Most-High. I gratefully express this peace everywhere I go. *And so it is!*

DAY 5

Having had a spiritual awakening, I now give from the Overflow of Life, pouring Itself out through me. *And so it is!*

DAY 6

Knowing that I only get to keep the infinite gifts of life when I share them with others, I say "yes" to this great Law of Life. *And so it is!*

DAY 7

As an ambassador of a Deeper Love Within, I accept the mandate to be the activity of God expressing Itself through me. *And so it is!*

AFTERWORD

Thank you for reading my book. It has taken me twenty-five years to say "yes" to this book, mainly out of fear and excuses as to why I shouldn't write.

A few years ago, when I started posting daily words of inspiration on Facebook, people kept asking me to put a book together. I then began to realize that if this book inspired at least one person's life, who then went on to inspire another person's life, it would be well worth the time and effort.

My prayer is that reading about my journey and spiritual transformation has opened your heart and mind to the Deeper Love Within you.

ABOUT THE AUTHOR

SHERMAN HARGRAVE served ten years in the U.S. Navy as a cook, then went on to study at the Culinary Institute of America. After graduating in 1991 and subsequently working at several major hotels, he opened his award-winning restaurant in San Diego, California: Sherman's Cajun and Creole Buffet. From 1997 to 2003 he employed numerous recovering addicts and alcoholics, fresh out of treatment programs, thus giving them a second chance to succeed in the workforce.

After walking away from his successful restaurant business, Sherman dedicated his life to a metaphysical approach he discovered for recovery. To pursue this course of action, he moved to Los Angeles in 2004 to study at the Agape University in Culver City and also took online courses at The University of Metaphysics.

As someone who has overcome twenty years of the horrors of addiction and who has been actively involved in his own recovery and the recovery of others, Sherman truly earned the right to talk about this wonderfully new and exciting approach to recovery. He has spent the last twenty-five years of his life teaching courses and facilitating seminars in prisons, alcohol and drug treatment centers, and at various military facilities.

The father of one son, Sherman now lives in Cebu City, Philippines, where he writes books and continues his metaphysical practice.

www.ingramcontent.com/pod-product-compliance
Lightning Source LLC
Chambersburg PA
CBHW061654040426
42446CB00010B/1736